Living in Religious Diversity: A Possibility for Malawi Muslim and Christian co-existence

Copyright 2020 by Anderson J M Mnthambala

All rights reserved, No part of this publication may be reproduced, stored in a retrieval system, or transmitted in any form or by any means, electronic, mechanical, photocopying, recording or otherwise, prior permission from the publishers.

Published by
Kachere Series
P.O. Box 1037, Zomba
ISBN: 978-99960-25-35-8

The Kachere Series is represented outside Africa by
African Books Collective, Oxford (orders@africanbookscollective.com)

Layout & Cover Design: Josephine Kawejere

Living in Religious diversity: A possibility for Malawi Muslim and Christian co-existence

Anderson J M Mnthambala (Rev)
L.Th.,Dip.B.TH,BA.Hons,PGD,MA

Kachere Books no. 75

Kachere Series
Zomba
2020

Kachere Series
P.O. Box 1037, Zomba, Malawi
Kachere@globemw.net
http://www.kachereseries.org.

This book is part of the Kachere Series, a range of books on religion, culture and society from Malawi. Other related Kachere titles so far are:

John Lloyd Lwanda, *Kamuzu Banda of Malawi: A Study in Promise, Power and Legacy, Malawi under Dr. Hastings Kamuzu Banda (1961-1994)*

Rhodian G. Munyenyembe, *Christianity and Socio-Cultural Issues: The Charismatic Movement and Contextualization in Malawi*

James Tengatenga, *The UMCA in Malawi: A History of the Anglican Church*

Isaac C. Lamba, *Contradictions in Post-War Education Policy Formulation and Application in Colonial Malawi 1945-1961: A History Study of the Dynamics of Colonial Survival*

Anthony Nazombe, *Operations and Tears: A New Anthology of Malawian Poetry*

Kapya John Kaoma,. *God's Family God's Earth: Christian Ecological Ethics of Ubuntu*

Kings M Phiri ed...*Malawi in Crisis: The 1959/60 Nyasaland State of Emergency and its Legacy*

The Kachere Series is the publication arm of the Department of Theology and Religious Studies of the University of Malawi

Series Editors: Dr. I. S. Mohammad; Dr. J. Thipa; Dr. H. Mvula; Dr D. Dembo, Dr Fr. Chaima, Mr. M. Mbewe, Mr. R. Mdoka

PREFACE

Both Christianity and Islam are missionary religions. Unless there is some agreement on the mode of evangelisation there is always the possibility that clashes between the adherents of these religions can occur. One is reminded of the jihads on the part of the followers of Islam as a religion and crusades on the part of the followers of Christianity as a religion. It is against this background that any discussion of possible peaceful relations between Islam and Christianity is very welcome. This book by the Rev A J Mnthambala is one such book which deals with this very important topic.

This book is about policy changes in Nkhoma Synod of Church of Central Africa Presbyterian regarding evangelism amongst Muslems. In Nkhoma Synod the areas where Moslems live have been divided into two zones, namely, the Lakeshore and Upland zones respectively. The Lakeshore zone covers the area from Nkhotakota down to Mangochi. The Upland zone covers the area from Lilongwe East down to Dedza North-west. The discussion in this book is focused on the Upland zone. The choice of the zone is deliberate because the policy changes are well exemplified in this area. Two policies in the synod's relationship with Islam have been identified and these policies are, 'antagonistic' approach and 'dialogue' approach. The implementations of these policies are reflected in different periods of the Church. The history of the Nkhoma Synod in relation to these policies is divided into four periods as follows: period characterised by emphasis on conversion (1889-1920); period of strategizing (1920-1950); period of African missionaries (1950-1962); period of Neighbours Mission (1962-2007). The year 2007 is simply the year when this work was submitted as a Master's dissertation.

The evangelistic approach during the first three periods from 1889 to 1962 was generally an antagonistic one. The approach changed when the Christian Council of Malawi (now known as Malawi Council of Churches) adopted an approach to Muslims known as Programme for Christian-Muslim Relations (PROCMURA) which was advocated by All Africa Conference of Churches (AACC). Through the Malawi Council of Churches a number of ministers in Nkhoma Synod were sent for studies in Christian-Muslim relations in Nigeria and other places. One of these ministers was Rev Michael Kajawa who eventually became a pastor of the Upland zone. Other measures taken by Nkhoma Synod to strengthen mission work amongst Muslims include the establishment of a Muslim Mission Desk at Synod offices and the adoption of a programme known as Neighbour Mission.

This book is significant for a number of reasons. Firstly it provides a case study of a success story of the implementation of 'dialogue' approach to evangelism amongst Muslims. Secondly the book outlines guidelines of how to implement 'dialogue' model of evangelism. Lastly it discusses some historical models of Christian-Muslim relationships.

By
Very Rev. Dr. Flex Chingota.
Retired Moderator of CCAP General Assembly,
Retired Chairperson of Public Affairs Committee,
Retired Lecturer at the University of Malawi (Chancellor College) is currently teaching at Blantyre University.

DEDICATION

I dedicate this book to my late parents Joseph and Folita Mngombe whose personality gave me life's most valuable treasures of life with Godly love and sacrifice. Their untiring pieces of advice have taught me the art of perseverance and hard work this far under the grace of God. May their souls live in peace.

Acknowledgements

I wish to express my sincere gratitude to all those who have contributed in any way to the successful completion of this book on Christian – Muslim relations in Malawi; with insight from CCAP Synod of Nkhoma, areas of Dedza North-West and Lilongwe east in the Central Region. It is not easy to thank all individuals who in various ways have made this book come to completion; like all Ministers, Elders, members of Women's Guild, Christians, Sheiks, and Muslims that I met and from whom I heard views on Muslim – Christian relations and whose experiences have been helpful in compilation of this book.

My sincere thanks go also to all the staff members in the Department of Theology and Religious Studies at Chancellor College, staff members of Kachere Research Center and Kachere Series, Zomba Theological College and Josophat Mwale Theological Institute Libraries for technical support in the process.

My special thanks go to Prof. Dr J.C. Chakanza and Prof. Dr Klaus Fiedler for the continued assistance they rendered at every stage of the book. I sincerely appreciate their constructive criticisms throughout the period of writing the book. A mention of Mr. Francis Perekamoyo must be made for providing his car when conducting field research work in the area of study.

I thank the CCAP Nkhoma Synod for allowing me to write such a book with regard to the mission work that is growing everyday under Neighbour Mission (among Muslims), with a moderate attitude. By taking the example of PROCMURA approach, whose method demands clear understanding of other faith communities, if you want to engage in interfaith dialogue.

A word of thanks must be extended to the selected congregations of the Synod of Nkhoma CCAP for the great cooperation, encouragement and the moral support received in particular, ministers and members, who willingly provided information that I needed for this book. The same is true of the support the sheikhs and Muslim members gave in the area, for their willingness to share with me the vital information that I was looking for.

Lastly, I thank friends and family members for their encouragement, not forgetting my dear wife Elestina and the children – Ulemu and her husband Stephen Chibophe and grandsons Yankho, Linga and Zaitwa; Jositino and his spouse Eliza and granddaughter Neta (Elestina jnr) and Anderson (Jnr) for their moral support. Above all I thank God for granting all the necessary facilities to get this book to its completion.

Introduction

This book has traced and examined the interaction between Christians and Muslims in the areas of Dedza North-West and Lilongwe East, the Nkhoma Mission area in the Central Region in Malawi. Firstly, it gives a brief history of the coming of Islam and Christianity to Malawi with an emphasis on Nkhoma Synod, which led to a situation in which the majority of the people of the area are Christians, with a sizable minority of Muslims, both along Lakeshore from Nkhotakota down to Mangochi and in the uplands of Dedza North –West and Lilongwe East.

Secondly, the book has examined the relationship between Christians and Muslims over the early missionary period with its emphasis on conversion (1889 – 1920), the strategizing mission work period (1920-1950), the period of indigenous missionary work (1950-1962) and the period of consolidation of the mission work under the Neighbour Mission to date, the period in which the Programme for Christian – Muslim Relations in Africa (PROCMURA)'s approach has been applied. Including principles and guidelines to interfaith dialogue in situations of religious diversity.

Through history to the present day situation, the book establishes the principles which have guided and are guiding interfaith dialogue in the area, by relating these approaches to the current thinking on relationship between Christianity and other faith communities. Here special prominence is given to the "moderate" PROCMURA approach, and the mutual perceptions and relationships between Muslims and Christians have been analyzed through interviews and group discussions of members of both Mosques and CCAP congregations.

This book presents both the approach and the work of PROCMURA as it relates to Malawi. PROCMURA's approach to Christian – Muslim relations is echoed in the work of the Neighbour Mission of the CCAP Nkhoma Synod, and its achievements are described.

It is the intention that this book may help to remove the fear of Christians that Islam is expanding very fast in Malawi and the perception of some Muslims that Christianity is dominating in most issues over the Muslim minority in Malawi. To help in this process suggestions are made on how dialogue between Muslims and Christians can be conducted that both communities can grow in respect and understanding on how they may address current issues concerning them both, like the HIV and Aids pandemic, gender issues to mention a few.

Contents

Preface	V
Dedication	**vii**
Acknowledgements	viii
Introduction	1
List of Abbreviations	6

Chapter One:

Mission to all — 7

1.1. Procmura's Origins	7
1.2. The Mission Concept	7
1.3. Historical Models for Understanding people of other faith communities	12
1.4. Inter-faith approach.	18
1.5. Procmura's teaching	21
1.6. Procmura's goal	23
1.7. Procmura's in Malawi	26
1.8. The future of Procmura's	28
1.9. The challenges of the future	32

Chapter Two:

Procmura is introduced to Malawi Council of Churches. — 36

2.1. Introduction	36
2.2. Christian, Muslim relations desk established	41
2.3. History of Christian Muslim Relations	41
2.4. Malawi Interfaith Aids Association (MIAA)	42

2.5. Conclusion ... **43**

Chapter Three:

Interfaith dialogue in CCAP Nkhoma Synod 1889-2007 ... **46**

3.2. A new wave to mission ... 47
3.3. The Fruits of mission to Muslims ... 52
3.4. Salvation outside the visible church ... 56
3.5. Neighbour mission ... 60
3.6. Interfaith reflections of dialogue ... 64

Chapter Four:

Living in Diversity: a possibility for Christians and Muslims of Dedza North -West and Lilongwe East in Peace ... **68**

4.1. Overview ... 68
4.2. Christian Muslim relations on obligation ... 70
4.3. Relationships ... 76
4.4. Nkhoma Synods admission policy ... 85
4.5. Witnessing for the religion ... 86
4.6. The ideal method ... 89
4.7. Conflict resolution ... 90
4.8. The basis for unity ... 95

Chapter Five:

Dialogue a prerequisite for peaceful co-existence for Malawian Muslims and Christian ... **108**

5.1. Introduction ... 108
5.2. Inter-faith dialogue ... 110
5.3. Communication as a catalyst ... 112
5.4. Methods to effective communication ... 113
5.5. Missions ... 114
5.6. Guidelines to dialogue ... 117

Chapter Six:

Conclusion **126**

Bibliography 128

List of abbreviations.

AACC	All Africa Conference of Churches
AGM	Annual General Meeting (MCC)
IMC	International Missionary Council
PROCMURA	Programme for Christian – Muslim Relations in Africa
CCM	Christian Council of Malawi
CCAP	Church of Central Africa Presbyterian
MCC	Malawi Council of Churches
MCP	Malawi Congress Party
UDF	United Democratic Front
IAP	Islam in Africa Project
ELC	European Liaison Committee
IIEC	Islam in Europe Committee
AFORD	Alliance for Democracy
CE	Common Era

Chapter One

Mission to All

1.1 PROCMURA's Origins.

Both Islam and Christianity are regarded as foreign to Africa as both are missionary religions. The presence of these religions aroused the idea of how they would relate to each other especially in the wake of political change in Africa when African nationalist movements were geared to obtain independence from colonial rule.[1] This was evident especially with the high sense of nationalism as leaders of the nationalist movements preached the need for constructive relationships and co-operation across the diverse linguistic, ethnic, religious and cultural frontiers.[2]

Churches were aware that Christianity was often seen as the religion of the colonialists, and the presence of missionaries was seen as a symbol of the continuing reality of colonialism. This led churches to consider how they would accomplish the 'three-self' thus self-governing, self-supporting, and self-propagating as worked out by Henry Venn (1796-1873) and Rufus Anderson (1796-1880) once independence was achieved in African countries.

"It was in the area of self-propagation of the Gospel that the seed of PROCMURA was sown."[3] The churches were aware that post-colonial African nations would evolve and that many of them would have both Christian and Muslim citizens. Therefore, the need for Christian – Muslim engagement as fellow citizens would be imperative. This became prominent with the changing political and religious climate in the African continent. The question that arose was "what would be the role of the church in such a climate?"

---

[1] PROCMURA, Theme: Witnessing in Religious Pluralistic Landscape in Africa, Strategic Plan 2007/8 - 2011/12, p. 6.
[2] Ibid.
[3] Ibid.

Light in the tunnel came in sight at the last International Missionary Council (IMC) Assembly held in Accra, Ghana. In November, 1957 African churches were strongly represented at this conference.[4] At the meeting the need for more intensive study of Islam was expressed for an action plan on how the churches would approach Islam and Muslims in Independent Africa. Two months after that Assembly, in January 1958, 'All Africa Church Conference' held a meeting in Ibadan, Nigeria with the theme "The Church in a Changing Africa." And a Special attention was given to the issue of 'Islam' raised at Accra two months before.

The Anglican Bishop of Ondo in Nigeria, S.O. Odutola, delivered a paper entitled, "Islam as it affects life in Nigeria" with emphasis on the issues discussed in Ghana. The question centered on, "how Christians in Africa need to interpret the Gospel in a more meaningful way to Muslims without violating the principle of good neighbourliness"[5]. The conference resolved that the church, as it ventures to preach Christ, should avoid medieval polemic responses to Islam which led to the crusades. Therefore, in order to avoid confrontation, the conference concluded that adequate and objective study of Islam and informed knowledge of the history of Muslims in the continent was imperative.[6]

It was obvious that the churches in Africa lacked expertise to attend to such a programme. Theological studies at the time had little to say about Islam and if there was any knowledge it was either clouded in ignorance or contained medieval polemical presentations and responses to Islam. The blanket image of Islam as a religion of violence and the perception of Muslims as enemies of Christianity remained strong in many circles then, as it still does in many Christian hearts today.

---

[4] PROCMURA, Theme: Witnessing in Religious Pluralistic Landscape in Africa, Strategic Plan 2007/8 - 2011/12, p. 7.
[5] Ibid.
[6] PROCMURA, Theme: Witnessing in Religious Pluralistic Landscape in Africa, Strategic Plan 2007/8 - 2011/12, p. 3.

This emphatically revealed the need to have a programme to particularly focus on Christian – Muslim relations in Africa. Then, International Missionary Council arranged a meeting in September 1958 in Oegstgeest in the Netherlands where representatives from different countries in Europe met.[7]

They facilitated a consultation with twenty missionary leaders in attendance. The theme was "Islam in Africa Project." It met to discuss how Europe could be of help to African churches to achieve an appropriate approach to Islam. Concurrently, a similar meeting was also taking place at Hartford, Connecticut in the United States of America to decide what help the American churches could offer to the African churches in the implementation of their quest for an appropriate approach to Islam.[8]

The Oegstgeest consultation resolved to send an emissary on a fact-finding mission to Africa to find out exactly what the churches were looking for. Thus, Pièrre Benignus of Paris Missionary Council was mandated to visit Africa on a fact-finding mission. He visited both countries in East and West Africa and reported back. This resulted in the founding of the Islam in Africa Project (IAP) in 1959 whose inauguration ceremony took place in Accra in Ghana. The central base of operations was Ibadan in Nigeria. Therefore, PROCMURA's birth involved Europeans, North Americans and Africans who together continued to nurse the child into maturity and now support its adult life. What a symbol for the Trinity.

The missionary members that assembled at the Oegstgeest consultation formed the European Liaison Committee (ELC) of PROCMURA. In conclusion we would say PROCMURA's seed was sown at Accra in Ghana in December, 1957, watered in Ibadan in January, 1958, nurtured in Oegstgeest in September, 1958 and transplanted as an African continental organization in 1959.

---

[7] Ibid.
[8] Ibid.

2.1.1 Name Change and Location

At the IAP meeting held in Nigeria in 1976 the question of location of IAP headquarters was discussed. After a deep consultation it was agreed to move from Ibadan to Nairobi, Kenya, where the headquarters offices of the All Africa Conference of Churches (AACC) are located, so it was viable to be near them. The implementation of that project took place in 1977. When the executive committee met in Nairobi in 1978, it resolved to change the name to Project for Christian – Muslim Relations in Africa (PROCMURA). These changes affected even the leadership of the organization. Since the establishment of the programme the leadership has been in the hands of either Americans or Europeans.

But a new wave came in the year 2000 when the first African was appointed as the General Advisor by the name Rev Dr Johnson A. Mbillah, a Ghanaian, succeeding the last white man called Stuart E. Brown, a lay Canadian. Further, when the general council of PROCMURA met at Abakobi near Accra in 2003 it decided to change the name to Programme for Christian – Muslim Relations in Africa because a project has a short span of life while a programme has longer life with expansion throughout Africa and so the latter was preferred and this has been gazetted by the authorities of the Kenyan government. This reveals the development of the Programme which has gone through to reach this far.[9]

1.2 The Mission Concept

When we talk of mission to Muslims, there are three approaches to dialogue. What is dialogue in the context of evangelism? In fact for the past thirty years, theological reflections on Christianity and other religions appear to be in three forms namely: - pluralism, exclusivism and inclusivism. This raises the whole question of dialogue with people of other faith communities.

---

[9] PROCMURA, Theme: Witnessing in Religious Pluralistic Landscape in Africa, Strategic Plan 2007/8 - 2011/12, pp. 6-9.

Dialogue refers to two parties meeting together discussing issues of common interest for the benefit of both sides. This could either be business or faith related issues as for our purpose. Such dialogue has to be contextual in order to be real. In dialogue, two parties meet to discuss understanding each others' religion and beliefs and appreciate that the other exists and so living in diversity peacefully does not become strange.[10]

In other words, in faith related issues, dialogue is an attempt by the church to act in partnership with those outside its institution to promote the Kingdom of God, with effects on the renewal of societies to manifest the values of the Kingdom, which include love, justice, freedom and truth. It is from these values that peace proceeds.[11] Raymond Fung proposes that partnership with the world as a model for evangelization is a new language based on an ecumenical strategy for Christian witness as partnership such that a congregation partners with people of the community.[12] This understanding assumes that partners are equal because they know their limits and limitations. Each partner realizes that without others he/she cannot succeed, and does not do things for the partner but he expects the other partner to do his or her share.

That means they share gain or loss, joy and sorrow. In addition, a partner has his own favourable agenda, but does not impose it on other partners.[13] That means partners are due to share their agenda with one another and so they are in dialogue. Therefore, the recognition of partnership compels them to explain their

---

[10] Arnold C. Temple and Johnson Mbillah (eds.), *Christianity and People of other Faith Communities*, Africa Church Information Service (ACIS) Printing Press, 2001, p. 2.
[11] Ibid. p. 2-3.
[12] Ibid. p. 2-3.
[13] Arnold C. Temple and Johnson A. Mbillah (eds.), *Christianity and People of other Faith Communities*, Africa Church Information Service (ACIS) Printing Press 2001, p. 24.

convictions to each other honestly and humbly.[14] Furthermore, partners are answerable to one another and mutually accountable.

A partner serves his or her fellow partners beyond the call of duty as the need arises.[15] The crucial questions to ask for this approach are- (i) why has God manifested himself in so many ways among different peoples? (ii) Do I have anything at all to learn from other peoples` understanding?[16] The answer can be - God is God of cultures and so it is our arrogance and feeling of superiority that cause us to answer in the negative. Therefore, it must be noted that: - "We cannot co-exist in our societies and decide to ignore each other. For better or for worse we are bound to relate and if we should relate positively we must understand each other."[17]

1.3 Historical models for understanding people of other faith Communities.

Before discussing the PROCMURA's approach, it is helpful to understand the views of other people from a historical perspective. There were and have been various views from where the present understanding has developed.

Paul Knitter outlines possible attitudes of Christians to other faith communities as follows:

2.3.1 conservative evangelical model.

In this group the teaching that prevails is that there is no room for dialogue; it is either one accepts Jesus as Lord and Saviour or not. That means Christian scripture can only measure faith systems and so dialogue is not accepted. A model of this kind, as an example, took place in Germany. They were responding to the attitude of the ecumenical movement towards other religions which was seen as a fundamental crisis in the Christian faith as part of liberalism and

---

[14] Ibid.
[15] Ibid.
[16] Ibid. p. 25.
[17] Ibid.

syncretism. Therefore, when some Evangelicals met in March 1970 in Frankfurt, Germany, they stated their position in regard to the attitude of the ecumenical movement towards other religions. They declared, "that other faith systems could only be evaluated with the yardstick of the Christian scripture i.e. dialogue is rejected as a prostitution of the Gospel."[18]

Further, Karl Barth, an advocate of the above view, says, "Religion is unbelief, it is a concern, indeed, we must say that it is the one great concern, of godless man."[19] Karl Barth, "looks at religion as human beings do, attempting to do what only God in Christ can do and has done and affirms that God's revelation in Jesus Christ is the only starting and ending point."[20]

2.3.2 Lausanne congress.

The moderate evangelicals who met four years later (1974) in Lausanne, Switzerland, were more evangelical in favour for openness to other faiths than those that met in Frankfurt in Germany. As a result they were more conciliatory and so recognized the need for a kind of dialogue that listens sensitively in order to understand the other person's faith so that he can be converted. That means the process of 'dialogue' is looked at as an instrument of conversion. It is a process of knowing one another in terms of other faith communities.[21]

2.3.3 Mainline protestant model.

This model agrees that revelation of God in other religions is possible but that there is no salvation. Tillich calls this "general revelation", Althaus calls it "original revelation", Brunner calls this,

---

[18] John H. Leith (ed.), *Creeds of the Churches, 'A Reader in Christian Doctrine from the Bible to the Present*, Westminster: John Knox Press, 1982, pp. 683-696. (The Frankfurt Declaration as quoted in Paul Knitter).
[19] Karl Barth, *Church Dogmatics*, vol. 1, p. 327.
[20] Ibid.
[21] Arnold C. Temple and Johnson A. Mbillah (eds.), *Christianity and People of other Faith Communities*: Africa Church Information Service (AICS) Printing Press, 2001, p. 27.

"creation revelation." Pannenberg states: "Any claim to superiority or normativity in Christian revelation cannot stand until it is verified through a dialogue with the revelation found in other world religions."[22] Althaus sums up to say: "Outside of Christ there is indeed a self-manifestation of God; therefore knowledge of God, but that does not lead to salvation, to union between God and human beings."[23]

2.3.4 Catholic model.

The Catholic model reminds us of the request that Pope John XXIII made when he asked Cardinal Bea regarding the position of the church to people of other faiths, in particular to Muslims. In the historic document the church affirmed that all peoples of the earth with their various religions form one community; therefore, the church respects the spiritual, moral and cultural values of these, Islam inclusive.[24] They adore one God, maker of heaven and earth, whom Abraham worshiped and with whom the Islamic faith is pleased to associate despite the fact that they do not revere Jesus but take him just as one of the prophets. They also honour Mary the mother of Jesus and sometimes call on her in devotion. They wait upon Judgment day when God will give each man his dues after resurrection. In fact, they teach about moral life, worshiping God through fasting, almsgiving and prayer. Despite the hostilities and quarrels between Christians and Muslims over centuries the Synod stated, "This sacred synod urges all to forget the past and strive sincerely for mutual understanding. On behalf of all mankind, let them make common cause of safe-guarding and fostering social justice, moral values, peace and freedom." This makes an open window for dialogue without compromise, affirming the universality of grace and salvation.

---

[22] Ibid.
[23] Ibid. p. 28.
[24] Ibid. p. 65.

2.3.4.1 Vatican's declaration on the relationship of the Church to Non-Christian religions.

Later, Pope Paul was ready for implementation[25] of the decree by setting up a secretariat headed by Cardinal Paolo Marella on 17th May, 1964, 'Relations with non-Christian religions'. Their discussions emphasized Unity and Love among men because all peoples comprise a single community, of one origin, created by God with their final goal in God.[26]

2.3.4.2 Resolution endorsed.

The resolution made towards Muslims after consultations states,

> "Upon the Muslims, too, the church looks with esteem. They adore one God, living and enduring, merciful and all powerful, maker of heaven and earth and speaker to men. They submit wholeheartedly ... just as did Abraham, with whom the Islamic faith is pleased to associate itself.
>
> Though they do not acknowledge Jesus as God they revere him as prophet ... they honour Mary, His virgin mother ... call on her in devotion. They wait upon the Day of judgment ... they prize moral life, and give worship to God ... through prayer, almsgiving and fasting. Although ... through centuries many quarrels and hostilities have arisen between Christians and Muslims, this most sacred Synod urges all to forget the past and to strive ... for mutual understanding. On behalf of all mankind let them make common cause of safe-guarding and fostering social justice, moral values and freedom."

This was announced on 28th October in 1965 in Rome at St. Peter's Square,[27] thus laying down foundations for dialogue.

---

[25] Walter M. Abbot, S.J., *The Documents of Vatican II*, New York: The America Press, 1966, p. 660.
[26] Ibid. pp. 663-668.
[27] Ibid. p. 663.

Through the influence of Karl Rahner, Vatican II affirms the universality of grace and salvation. Karl Rahner, who had been influential in the preparation of the document called 'Lumen Gentium', optimistically calls for understanding of the divine salvific will of God. If God has the desire to save all humankind, He will do it. He further adds that to think negatively of humanity is to underestimate God's love and grace. Therefore, in his theory of anonymous Christianity he states,

> "Christ is the absolute perfection and guarantee of God's love and grace - i.e. he is the final constitutive case for salvation."[28]

Hans Küng, a Roman Catholic theologian, sees Rahner's position as theological fabrication and argues for a Theo-centric as opposed to a Christo-centric or Ecclesio-centric approach to the understanding of salvation in dialogue with other faith communities.[29]

2.3.5 Parallelism of the Copernican revolutionary model.

John Hicks' model parallels with the Copernican model that is compared to the universe and the sun in the center with planets revolving around it to that of faith experience. Where God is taken to be in the center and all religions revolving around him in the same way as the planets revolve around the sun. This is considered the most radical model for the understanding of other faiths and not compatible with Christianity. In Christianity Jesus Christ is taken as the way, the truth and the life by Christians and that through him man is reconciled to God.

2.3.5.1 Unitive pluralism of religions.

This implies that all religions are equally valid. In this context Jesus is seen as one among many in a world of saviours and revealers; a view found unacceptable among Christians. It threatens the

---

[28] Arnold C. Temple and Johnson A. Mbillah (eds.), *Christianity and People of other Faith Communities*, p. 29.
[29] Ibid. p. 30.

traditional self-understanding of Christianity, which is unique, exclusive, superior, definitive, normative and absolute. Whatever our answer may be, one thing is clear, being judgmental of other religions is not the genuine Christian position of faith seeking understanding. "We fail to do justice to other religions when we apply Christian criteria and categories to assess them."[30]

2.3.6 An authentic African model for Africa.

"Africa possesses a spirituality of wholeness."[31] Arnold Temple proposes a model of dialogue in the African context as an engagement for the promotion of the Kingdom of God in our midst that seeks to remove all forms of injustice and to promote a new humanity. Such a dialogue with our faith systems that enables openness and genuine listening enables our religions to inform and strengthen each other. The objective of dialogue in Africa should be that of promotion of tolerance and eradication of intolerance. This would promote peaceful co-existence in spite of differences and ensuring equal opportunities for all in all facets of life.

Hans Küng puts it this way,

> "No peace among the people of the world without peace among religions. No peace among religions without dialogue between the religions. And there is no dialogue between the religions without accurate knowledge of one another."[32]

We can add that there will be no accurate knowledge of the other when we do not enter into conversation (dialogue) with each other. It must be noted that doctrinal debates will always keep us apart, whereas constitutive dialogue around vital issues of common social concern will achieve positive results, e.g. when dealing with issues

---

[30] Arnold C. Temple and Johnson A. Mbillah (eds.), *Christianity and People of other Faith Communities*, Africa Church Information Service (ACIS) Printing Press, 2001, p. 29.
[31] Ibid. p. 30.
[32] Ibid.

of the HIV and AIDS pandemic, the hunger crisis, orphans to mention a few. After looking at these various views, we now see how the position of PROCMURA has come about.

1.4 Inter-faith approach

2.4.1 Extreme left position.

This is an antagonistic approach sometimes called fundamentalistic or otherwise in either case of Islam or Christianity, where there is a total denial to accept the other as a true religion. By holding an antagonistic position one works against the other religion and under any circumstances tries to defeat the other. Examples can be the following

2.4.1.1 In Islamic circles.

Ahmed Deedat, a Muslim in Durban in South Africa, has established a center called 'Islamic Propagation Center International' that publishes a lot of literature and audio tapes for the propagation of the Islamic faith through literature and public debates between Christians and Muslims. Some literature is polemic and against the Christian faith.

This approach is seen in literature like: '50,000 Errors in the Bible,' 'Crucifixion or Cruci – Fiction,' 'What the Bible Says about Muhammad (PBUH),' 'Muhammad (PBUH) – The Natural Successor to Christ (PBUH)'; all these are works that may not be accepted in Christian circles because they are not compatible with the Christian Faith.

Some of Ahmed Deedat's literature refers to issues of alcohol entitled (i) 'Disease'? If alcoholism is a disease then it is the only disease that is sold in bottles, is advertised in newspapers ... propels one's health to self-destruction and destroys family life and increases crime, (ii) Dancing is sex pure and simple, and impure sex (iii) An anguished mother's plea – This is what happens when you marry outside religion!. His writings even defame the name of Jesus as a mere prophet and not the Son of God as understood and believed by Christians.[33]

His works have been answered by John Gilchrist, sometimes with words at the bottom of the front page of each booklet 'A refutation of ......!' e.g. "Crucifixion or Cruci-Fiction". John Gilchrist also from South Africa has responded in one of his writings entitled "The Crucifixion of Christ: A Fact, not Fiction" and at the bottom of the front page he writes, 'A refutation of the theory that Jesus plotted a coup and survived the cross'.[34]

2.4.1.2 In Christian circles.

Kuthino Fernandez, a charismatic preacher and founder of the Church "Armée de Victoire" in Kinshasa in the Democratic Republic of Congo preached against the Islamic faith in 1999 and burnt a Quran after it was handed over to him by a young man upon his conversion from Islam to Christianity. The Islamic community was offended. The event was transmitted both on radio and television owned by his Church. It became a conflict between all Christians of charismatic churches and the Muslims in Kinshasa. The police succeeded in preventing confrontations between the two religions. Kuthino was taken to a tribunal and convicted on the charge of mass incitement to violence. He spent several months in prison.[35]

2.4.2 Extreme right position.

In this group we have an example from Ghana of a church with a prophetess seeking a compromise approach for Christianity and Islam to co-exist peacefully. It takes a position where a Christian is taken as just another Muslim and vice-versa. An example is that of the "Zeta Healing Mission in Ghana" whose founder is a prophetess

---

[33] Ahmed Deedat, *Is the Bible God's Word?* Durban: IPCI, 1992, p. 15.
[34] John Gilchrist, *Crucifixion of Christ: A Fact, not Fiction*, Cape Town: Life Challenge, 1985, pp. 3-35.
[35] Arnold C. Temple and Johnson A. Mbillah (eds.), *Christianity and People of other Faith Communities*, Africa Church Information Service (ACIS) Printing Press, 2001, p. 83.

by the name of Lehem. The Church holds that, since Christianity and Islam trace their roots to Abraham, it is a sufficient reason for the two faiths to come together under the one roof of Zeta Healing Mission Church which cerebrates all Muslim and Christian festivals, and all its members clothe in white for worship. It is evident that this church has not made any real impression on the Ghanaian society.[36]

2.4.3 The moderate position.

This view is middle way between the two extremes and demands understanding of other faiths communities that leads to dialogue. Therefore, the theology underside of PROCMURA upholds and seeks a just and peaceful society for all in which case with freedom of religion where everyone practices his faith and co-exist with other faith in diversity. PROCMURA further believes the equality of all people that truth and love are of paramount importance values for peaceful co-existence. That means, mutual respect, good neighborliness and tolerance are acknowledged as critical components in the search for a peaceful, compassionate and just world.

The two major principles under this roof include:

(a) Being faithful and responsible in Christian witness in an environment of interfaith situations. This position demands faithfulness to Christian principles and the avoidance of compromise for the sake of peace. In any context, non-peace witness should be avoided such as bearing false witness in the name of scripture. One must make sure that the Gospel is Good News and does not become bad news. It is essential to take the context seriously when witnessing for Christ.

(b) Christians and Muslims must engage in conversation to promote peace and peaceful co-existence: This can be achieved by following the steps below, as both Muslims and Christians have the mandate

---

[36] Ibid.

to promote peace. The churches must be proactive to promote peace with their counterparts the Muslims.

1.5 PROCMURA's teaching

It is in the interest of PROCMURA that the church engages in dialogue as a means of evangelism by reminding the church to be faithful and responsible in interfaith situations by taking the context seriously. In order to prevent compromise, false witnessing must be avoided at any cost so that the Good news is always brought fourth.

There are many issues that Muslims do not understand in Christianity such as the issue of the Trinity. The Muslim finds it difficult to accept the doctrine of the Trinity. How can God be one, yet three persons? How can $1+1+1$ be 1? In reply, the arithmetic formula is not correct; rather it should be $1\times1\times1 = 1$. Secondly, the question of the Trinity must be understood as a mystery. With that understanding, we talk of God the Father as Creator, God the Son as Saviour and God the Holy Spirit who convicts an individual to bring about salvation. God the Father is seen in the creation story in Genesis, while Jesus Christ was born human to bring about salvation for sinful man, and the Holy Spirit manifested Himself on the day of Pentecost to guide the Kingdom of God.

Therefore, it is the task of the Church to make sure that in all areas where a Muslim is unable to draw out the truth, it should conduct an interpretation that suffices to draw out the Good News for the recipient. The Church should ensure that through training in specialized knowledge. Every member church of the Malawi Council of Churches should have a representative dealing with this specialized course in the ministry to Muslims. In addition this course should also be introduced in the churches' institutions to bring awareness and knowledge of Islam and how to share Christ with them.

This shall enhance the understanding of the Islamic faith, which enables us to better relate to them. Therefore, it is the third approach of the moderate view against antagonism and compromise that PROCMURA follows. Who understands the faith of the other is able to witness better because he or she is aware of the other person's faith. Such approach leads to dialogue and discussions for proper understanding of the counter-part.

2.5.1 Organization of PROCMURA.

When the Islam in Africa Project, later renamed PROCMURA, was founded as an African organization, it was supervised by committees, with the work being done mainly by Area Advisors. In the formation of these committees, caution was taken not to establish another missionary society or denominational body. Therefore, IAP became a federation of local Area Committees, with a Governing Council with a Council Chairman. The project staff, such as Area Advisors and General Advisor was seconded to IAP by their Churches but accountable to the Council. The European partners who were active in creating the IAP formed the Islam in Europe Committee (IIEC); later its name changed to European Liaison Committee (ELC). The aim was and still is to achieve a better understanding of Islam. The current members of the European Liaison Committee include the following:- The Protestant Church in The Netherlands, Dan Mission, The Church of Scotland, Presbyterian Church of Northern Ireland and most Protestant Churches in Europe.

The first General Advisor was Rev Tom Beetham who formulated the initial vision for the Islam in Africa Project, especially that it should not become another missionary society or denomination but rather an arm of the churches. The last European Advisor was Stuart R. Brown from Canada. It was only in 2000 that an African emerged as General Advisor by the name of Johnson A. Mbillah, currently in position in-charge of Programme for Christian Muslim Relations to date under the supervision of the General Council of PROCMURA. The General Council is the outstanding body that used to meet biannually, but since 1997 has changed to meet every four years. It comprises the following:- The Executive Committee, the staff and all chairpersons from all Area Committees and the General

Advisor, Regional coordinators, Women's Coordinator, Project Officer and Literature Consultant, who form part of the staff. This was followed by the appointment of Angele Dogbe as the first African Women's Education Coordinator. The North American and Canadian Protestant churches form another Liaison Committee.

1.6 PROCMURA's goal

The goal of PROCMURA was and still is to keep before the churches of Africa south of the Sahara the responsibility to understand Islam and the Muslims of their region. This would give churches the task of interpreting faithfully the Gospel of Jesus Christ in the Muslim world. This can be achieved only through the development of research and educational tools. In that context area committees have strategies to implement with partner organizations like the European Liaison Committee and North American Partners. The extent of PROCMURA's ability would be assessed by its fulfilling its primary mission by the following factors in the context of Christian – Muslim relations in Africa and by the nature of the relationship between PROCMURA and the member churches in the region.[37]

2.6.1 Impact of PROCMURA upon Churches in the Sub-Saharan region.

In general the relationship between Christians and Muslims in Africa is said to continue to be good and is built on the principle of 'respect and peaceful co-existence'. Probably this is based on a deeper African principle of mutual understanding and tolerance beyond religious borders.[38] While the faith communities live side by side, they do so with little exchange. This is more apparent in rural areas than in the large metropolitan areas of the continent.

Why, then, should there be deteriorating relationships between the two faiths like in Sudan and Nigeria? There are various views to answer this question. Some would say that the increased visibility

---

[37] F. Joseph Stammer and Sem Chipenda Dasonkho, Final Report - Evaluation of the Project for Christian – Muslim Relation in Africa, November 17, 1997.
[38] Ibid. p. 4.

of Islamic institutions in various parts of Africa or cohesion among Islamic countries by oil producing states would contribute to such deterioration. Others say that when religious, secular and political institutions of the West decreased their support to African countries, Islam increased to present itself as a counter to the status quo.

As a result, Islam is seen as taking advantage of deteriorating socio-economic situations by offering attractive incentives such as scholarships to Arab countries, food in times of hunger, etc to those willing to join. It is believed that Islamization of the whole of the African continent peacefully or by coercion is one of the main aims of Islam.[39] This is because many Christians in many countries feel besieged by Muslims' intolerance and are not sure how to respond. For example, in countries where there has been no open conflict, occasional clashes have been prompted by circulation of false information such as on radio attacking the Bible by Muslim extremists or vice-versa.[40] It is assumed that Muslims try to know us, to fight us better by seeking out our feeble points.[41] Therefore, PROCMURA's desire is love of Muslims and that it should not end in confusion. In this context, when we talk of the Programme for Christian – Muslim Relations in Africa, it must be understood that "Dialogue does not mean the rejection of Evangelism." However, through maintenance of a defensive and apologetic stance that denounces all forms of prejudice and injustice we can build respect and understanding between Christians and Muslims through acquiring a deeper knowledge of Islam and how to share Christ with our Muslim neighbours.[42]

---

[39] F. Joseph Stammer and Sem Chipenda Dasonkho, Final Report - Evaluation of the Project for Christian – Muslim Relation in Africa, November 17, 1997..
[40] Ibid. p. 5.
[41] Ibid. p. 5.
[42] F. Joseph Stammer and Sem Chipenda Dasonkho, Final Report-Evaluation of the Report for Christian – Muslim relations in Africa, November 17,1997. p. 5.

2.6.2 PROCMURA's mission.

PROCMURA has always and still adopts a low profile so that Muslims do not see it as an aggressive missionary organization. Therefore, PROCMURA needs to be seen as an advisory group or organization, assisting churches in Africa on Christian – Muslim relations. As a supporting organization for specific needs of the churches in Africa, it offers training in specialized knowledge with literature and financial support. It has the strategy to promote a better knowledge of Islam, to prevent undermining the Islamic faith and have an emphasis only on converting Muslims.[43] PROCMURA wants to be a consultant, a reminder or an encourager of unity in diversity that is a place where the members of the two religions are able to stay in peace while maintaining their respective faiths.[44] An example could be that of the area under study of Dedza North-West and Lilongwe East, the Nkhoma Mission Area where Muslims and Christians are able to maintain the unity in diversity.

2.7.2 The executive committee.

The Executive Committee operates on behalf of the General Council to monitor day to day activities when the General Council is not meeting, with key leaders comprising the Chairman and his Deputy, the General Advisor and four other members. The rest of the members rotate after every four years when the General Council is meeting except for the General Advisor whose post becomes vacant after every six years but is renewable upon satisfactory performance.

2.7.3 Regional coordinators.

There are of course efficiency purposes and so Africa is divided into regions to enable PROCMURA's work well coordinated at grassroots level to the central office by the Regional Coordinators. The Regional Coordinator is one of the Area Advisors but appointed by

---

[43] Ibid. p. 7.
[44] Ibid. p. 17.

the Executive Committee with recommendations from the General Advisor. The Regional Coordinator serves a period of three years renewable for one term of three years only. The person combines his/her regional work with that of Area Advisor. e.g. Regional Coordinator for the East and Central Africa region.

2.7.4 Area advisors.

They serve as contact persons for the churches in the area of operation to constructively engage Muslims and Christians to work towards peaceful co-existence; at the same time they operate as channels of ideas and experiences on the subject matter in a given country or area. Further, they assist Area Committees to organize programmes on Christian – Muslim relations in their respective countries or areas of work. They are consultants for the Area Committee within their respective National Christian Councils. As by 30th January, 1999 there were around twenty Area Committees operating at various levels of effectiveness: e.g. - the Gambia, Cote d'Ivoire, Ghana, Burkina Faso, Benin, Northern Nigeria, Western Nigeria in West Africa, while in East and Southern Africa Tanzania, Kenya and Sudan had Area Advisors.[45]

2.7.5 Registered trustees.

The General Council of PROCMURA appoints four and not more than six persons as Registered Trustees, who then hold all land and properties belonging to PROCMURA. The names of these four are incorporate into Programme for Christian – Muslim Relations in Africa Registered Trustees. With a seal which is kept in the custody of the General Advisor.

1.7. PROCMURA's work in Malawi

Since the establishment of PROCMURA, it did not take long for Malawi to become a member through the Christian Council of

---

[45] Ibid. F. Joseph Stammer and Sem Chipenda Dasonkho, Final report - Evaluation of the Project for Christian- Muslim relations in Africa, November 17, 1997, p. 17.

Malawi, now Malawi Council of Churches. There has always been a desire to own an Area Advisor. The first candidate was the late Rev.D.P.Gareta of CCAP Nkhoma Synod who was trained both in Kenya and the United States of America at Fuller Theological Seminary. Unfortunately, upon his return he died in a car accident. Despite the tragedy, the Area Committee continued to work hard to promote PROCMURA principles. At one time late M.J. Kajawa was an interim Advisor awaiting for a fully qualified person. He too was from CCAP Nkhoma Synod.

It was during this period that a number of candidates had attended various courses with the recommendations of the Area Committee. Late Rev I.S. Salimoni of Nkhoma Synod CCAP chaired the committee. Thereafter, late Rev Ted Mwambila and late Fr. Edgar Malunda (Anglican) had gone for further studies at Selly Oak Colleges at the Centre for Christian – Muslim Relations, an affiliate college of the University of Birmingham, graduating with a Certificate and Diploma respectively.

The author a member of CCAP Nkhoma Synod followed in 1997. He went to the same college in the United Kingdom for the 1997/98 academic year graduating with a Post Graduate Diploma.[46] The year 2001 saw late Fr. E.E. Malunda's appointment as the Area Advisor by the Malawi Council of Churches. He was to work with the Area Committee, on secondment by his church, the Anglican Upper Shire Diocese.[47] Therefore, the first meeting of the member church representatives was held at Chilema Lay Training Center on the 10th of October 2001, where a committee was instituted.

---

[46] Anderson J.M. M'nthambala, Study Tour Report 1997/98 Academic Year at Westhill College (University of Birmingham-UK) to Malawi Council of Churches, 30.10.1998.

[47] Bertha Kalagho, Minutes of Area Committee Meeting at Chilema CLTC 10th May, 2001.

1.8 The Future of PROCMURA.

When the General Council of PROCMURA met in Ethiopia in the year 1997, it made resolutions that could determine a successful future for the organization on the African continent by the help of its partners. Among the decisions, the following surfaced as important: decentralization, sustainability and operational structural communications.

2.9.1 Decentralization.

In order to decentralize the work, each Area Committee to develop a mission statement and strategic plan accordingly, by putting in place the needs and challenges of that particular area or region. This should be done by prioritizing the activities of the Area Committee that it wants to accomplish in a given year or years e.g. a five year period. In such contexts the witness to Islam should be built on the understanding of issues pertaining to Christian – Muslim relations in Africa. When Christian churches and Muslims are involved, the emphasis shall be on local training activities for interfaith religious dialogue with properly trained personnel.

2.9.2 Project's sustainability in Africa.

PROCMURA to look at the issues of sustainability in the context of Africa. Therefore, it would attempt to broaden the base contacts by involving Evangelicals, Roman Catholics and Pentecostals to develop together closer links with Muslims on common issues and goals. Another area of sustainability is to include training institutions to introduce Islam and Christian – Muslim relations on their curriculum so that the trained personnel shall be in a good position to multiply in training others accordingly.

Each Area Committee to recognize PROCMURA's mission and challenges for the sustainability of the Programme on the continent. It establishes scholarship programmes, for training to improve and help the churches' participation in selection and funding. In addition, establish African centers for training for degrees at undergraduate (BA, BDiv) and post-graduate (MA or

PhD) levels. In addition, literature and research programmes to develop publications for Africa and at the same time to have enough material for libraries. Such programmes not to deny participation of women and the youth. The whole issue is that churches in Africa should reach a stage where they shall be self-supporting from within Africa.

2.9.3 Improved operational and structural communications.

With improved communications the operation to enhance the ability to support and coordinate activities of all areas. The committees both at area and continental level continue to develop towards achieving autonomous status. This development of relations between National Councils on the continent aims at creation of smaller units such that two countries may form an area committee. This is so to create efficient communication channels between Area Advisors and the General Advisor.[48]

2.9.4 Result of PROCMURA.

PROCMURA to broadens its ground base and deepens the level of participation through systematic recruitment strategies. By following all scholarship recipients upon completion of their training to encourage them apply and put into practice the knowledge acquired. In addition, PROCMURA proposes altering funding strategy for short and long term such as three years funding commitments to ease the donor's participation. This includes establishing income generating activities. Procmura encourages proper financial reporting systems for easy assessment of proper management and transparency.[49]

---

[48] Oduyoye Modupe: Decision of the Executive Committee of PROCMURA on the Evaluation of the Project for Christian – Muslim relations at 38th PROCMURA Meeting, minutes 1997-11:24-25.

[49] Oduyoye Modupe: Decision of the Executive Committee of PROCMURA on the Evaluation of the Project for Christian – Muslim relations at 38th PROCMURA Meeting, minutes 1997-11:24-25, p. 7.

2.9.5 Materialization of 1997 general council resolutions.

Since 1977, substantial development has taken place in relation to the resolutions made by the General Council. One of these is the completion of the strategic plan for 2007/08 -2011/12. The document was presented before a partner's workshop that took place in Nairobi, Kenya in January 2006 where some liaison committee members both from Europe and North America were present. Together with Regional and Area Advisors, Women Representatives from all countries concerned were available. The document is now complete for the next five years. The first African lady as the Women's and Education Programme Coordinator,[50] Rev Angele Dogbe from Togo, was also present. The intensification of youth and church leaders programmes was emphasized as an issue for advancement. The appointment of the first African General Advisor, Rev Dr Johnson A. Mbillah, a Ghanaian, was of a great achievement in the history of PROCMURA. They both had been trained by PROCMURA.[51] Johnson A. Mbillah has retired is currently replaced by Adrake Kom Dzinyefa as the new General Adviser of PROCMURA from Togo beginning from January, 2020.[52]

2.9.5.1 Some other achievements.

The Programme for Christian – Muslim Relations in Africa has so far done the following issues that needs a mention. The dissemination of information on Islam and Christian – Muslim Relations in African to churches and mission organizations, both in Anglophone and Francophone West Africa and Anglophone East and Southern Africa. New ventures are looked into in North Africa and countries in the SADC region with exception of Malawi, an already member of the programme in the region. Therefore, the emphasis at

---

[50] PROCMURA, *Strategic Plan 2007/08 – 2011/12*, AACC Printing Press, p. 4.

[51] They were both trained by PROCMURA. Johnson A. Mbillah is a Ghanaian, Angele Dogbe, a minister with an MA Degree in Christian – Muslim relations comes from Togo.

[52] Rev. Dr. Adrake Kom Dzinyefa is a minister of the Evangelical Presbyterian church of Togo who had been PROCMURA's Area Adviser in Togo for some time..

grassroots ministry of faithful and responsible Christian witness is encouraged through training, seminars and workshops at area levels. And Collaboration between Christians and Muslims has been initiated for peace and peaceful co-existence.

The programme has directly or indirectly influenced Christian – Muslim relations in Africa on issues of mutual interest and concern. PROCMURA makes sure that discussions on interfaith-dialogue take place where conflict arises between communities. By getting involved in peace initiatives where political, religious and ethnic issues deeply divide Christians and Muslims.

In-order to achieve this, specialized training and research on Islam and Christian – Muslim relations in Africa to Masters or PhD levels for the home countries in Africa like Ghana is carried out.[53] Special mention of St. Paul's University, Limuru in Kenya needs to be made because it is where students can now study up to Masters Level, while at Mekane Yesu Seminary in Addis Ababa students can study up to Bachelor's degree on Islam and Christian – Muslim Relations as major subjects in the African context. Such courses used to take place outside Africa in America or Europe.

The desk of women's coordinator on Christian Muslim Relations in Africa provides a forum for Women to sharing experiences on issues of particular concern within Procmura headed by a lady pastors. In addition research on Islam and Christian – Muslim relations in the African context has been encouraged, documented and the findings have been published.[54] Furthermore, PROCMURA has published occasional papers e.g. "From the Cross to the Crescent" by Johnson Mbillah and John Chesworth (eds) in which

---

[53] John Azumah, *The Legacy of Arab-Islam in Africa: A Quest for Inter-religious Dialogue*, 2001.

[54] The quarterly *Newsletter* of the Programme for Christian – Muslim relations in Africa; Johnson A. Mbillah and John Chesworth, *From the Cross to the Crescent*. A PROCMURA Occasional Paper, ACIS Printing Press, 2004. Others are: Stuart Brown, *The Nearest in Affection – Towards a Christian Understanding of Islam*, Geneva: WCC, 1994; Arnold Temple and Johnson Mbillah, *Christianity and People of other Faiths*, ACIS 2000.

academic and practical matters on Christian – Muslim Relations are delt with. Further publications include *Christianity and People of other Faith Communities* by Arnold C. Temple and Johnson Mbillah (eds.), *The Nearest in Affection – 'Towards a Christian Understanding of Islam* by Stuart Brown, to mention just a few.[55]

1.9. The challenges of the future.

Despite the achievements PROCMURA has made, there is a lot ahead waiting for accomplishment. Some of these challenges include the following:

1. To start Master's programmes in Islam and Christian – Muslim Relations in two more theological colleges in Francophone and Anglophone West Africa. Limuru University in Kenya has started with Certificate, Diploma, Post Graduate Diploma and Masters Programmes and hopefully PhDs degrees respectively.

2. To promote and support women theologians to take studies in Islam seriously, so as to promote the Women's Programme. The Women's and Education Programme Coordinators go through the process, studying the subject.

3. To establish a PROCMURA research center.

4. To work towards establishing an Investment Fund for the programme. For example the Head office complex in Nairobi part of which is rented to raise funds today.56[56]

5. To look into the expansion of the work into Southern Africa, Central Africa and the Sahel region of Africa.

The wider challenges facing PROCMURA can be classified into four groups: political, economic, socio-cultural and technological. They can be highlighted as follows:-

---

[55] PROCMURA: *Strategic Plan 2007/8 – 2011/12 January*, 2006.

[56] .This is accomplished, the new Head Office is operational in Nairobi Kenya with other sections rented as fund raising activity.

2.10.1 Political challenges.

The biggest political challenge is the tendency to create tensions between Christians and Muslims. Terrorists tend to identify themselves with religious beliefs against political beliefs. Another problem is the multiplicity of religions coming to Africa and inter-religious organizations flocking to Africa and the competing world civilizations that want to own the African mind and the continent. These challenges face the African mind with often unstable political status.

2.10.2 Economic challenges.

The shifting donor funding priorities, especially the short-term character of much of the funding, reduce the sustainability of the programme in the areas of capacity building and advocacy. The poverty the churches experience in Africa makes them fail to carry out their own Christian – Muslim relations programmes. Urbanization results in increased movement of youths into the cities, increasing the number of slum dwellers and destitutes, which creates a challenge for PROCMURA. The destitute and slum dwellers find themselves in awkward situations of failing to sustain themselves physically while at the same time to be firm in their faith, let alone on how to relate to people of other faith communities. The churches lack resources to satisfy the many needs of these people, so they cannot support the Christian youth in such situations of pluralist religions and of economic obstacles.

2.10.3 Social and cultural challenges.

Another major challenge is that of religions becoming increasingly part of people's identity, sometimes leading to extremism. Christian – Muslim marriages and sensitivity of Islam are causing tension and may result in conflicts. In this situation of increased sensitivity, methods of evangelism adopted by some organizations with antagonistic tendencies may not go well with the principles of

PROCMURA.[57] The poor economic status of the churches leads to few people being trained in Christian – Muslim relations, so that there is a high level of illiteracy and misinformation.

The breakdown of the socio-cultural fabric is leading to a decline of moral values so that corruption and violence become the order of the day. An example is the rise of the HIV and AIDS pandemic affecting the whole world.[58]

2.10.4 Spread of the HIV and AIDS pandemic.

At the beginning of this millennium, the world is faced with various crises, the most challenging one being that of HIV and AIDS. This is continually destroying peoples, families, villages and cities and more so in Africa than in any other continent. And the most affected ones are women, young girls and children. The virus affects children at birth or during breast-feeding and this is drastically increasing every day; due to the low social status of women, subordination to men and common discrimination. These usually limit their opportunities of being informed of the pandemic. Women would be fearful of AIDS, desperate to protect themselves but lack of knowledge and cultural restrictions are disarming them. That is why social-cultural practices and conflicts are promoting the spread of the virus. The HIV and AIDS pandemic respects neither social status nor religious affiliation but affects everyone.

That is why PROCMURA decided together with Christian and Muslim women to offer an interfaith approach to deal with the pandemic. In that, Christian and Muslim women in the rural and enclosed areas are able to fight against the spread of the disease, against stigma and discrimination and for their right to live positively.

The work started with joint consultations with Christian and Muslim women in the constituencies of PROCMURA in sub-Saharan

---

[57] PROCMURA, *Strategic Plan 2007/08 – 2011/12*. p. 18.
[58] This becomes an issue in PROCMURA arising from consultations with both Christian and Muslim women and children in dialogue.

Africa, addressing and discussing the position of women, organizing knowledgeable women to support the lowly, creating awareness for VCT counseling. This would help them know their status and be able to break the silence.

2.10.5 Technological challenges.

Technology levels are still low in Africa, so that even some PROCMURA staff are computer illiterate. In addition, through the internet negative information about various religious communities is easily accessible.

In conclusion we would say that the issue of PROCMURA's approach is an issue of importance for the churches in Africa even beyond when we come to the issue of dealing with our neighbours, the Muslims. This is the approach that cherishes love and truth without compromise in witnessing for Jesus Christ.

Chapter Two

PROCMURA is introduced to Malawi Council of churches

Introduction

Africa is known for her Multi-religious scenario even before the coming of Islam and Christianity, the multi-religious aspect was still there within African Traditional Religion. In case of Malawi Islam was the first foreign religion to appear in the 1840's, famous for its trade in slaves, Ivory, animal skins and very little of evangelism. On the contrary Christianity followed with evangelism zeal beside commerce and civilization as a result of the recommendations by David Livingstone. That meant, the two religions found African Traditional Religion in the hearts of Africans already cherished before the advent of the former two religions. The partition of Africa by the European nations led missionaries into many parts of Africa to found churches. This was true Malawi then, Nyasaland e.g. the coming of Free Church of Scotland in 1875 under the leadership of Rev. Dr.Robert Laws, the Free Church of Scotland 1876 under the leadership of Henery Hendreson, the Dutch Reformed Church Mission from South Africa with William Murry and T.B.Vlok as leaders, Universities Mission to Central Africa in 1861 at Magomero with Bishop Mackenzie leading the group and the Roman Catholic Church in 1891 in Mangochi with the white fathers and later in1892 at Nzama in Tcheu district respectively. It was evident that the expansion of the church was crucial throughout the African continent.

During the 1950's the new political wind blew throughout Africa for liberation for independent states. The immediate question that needed an immediate answer was,

"How will the church operate in an environment of religious diversity?" in particular with Islam.
Secondly,

"How shall the church stand against such environment regarding self-governing, self-supporting and self-propagating?" [59]

This aroused the concept for good neighbourliness with other religious communities for peaceful co-existence in diversity. So, PROMURA then Islam Africa Project was born in 1959 to tackle the problem. Though, started small in West Africa but has since grown big throughout Africa with exception of some countries far north of Africa and in the SADC region. The Programme is now found in both Anglophone and Francphone countries in the West Africa and Francophone and Anglophone East Africa respectively with the General Adviser and executive committee working as management Team together with Area Committees through Christian Councils respectively.[60]

The establishment of interfaith dialogue's desk in Malawi

The birth of Malawi Area Committee on issues on Christian-Muslim Relations came into being at the Annual General Meeting of then Christian council of Malawi held at Namoni Katengeza Church Lay Training Center (then Chongoni) from 6- 8, November 1967. When, the issue of Islam Africa Project (IAP) was brought to light before the General Assembly by James Crossley from Nigeria. [61]

The council upon hearing this; was moved to participate in the venture. The two member churches, who showed great interest, were Diocese of Malawi and Nkhoma Synod CCAP. Then, the Council, in January 1970, sent three ministers in the names of Rev. Fr. J.A.Lunda, A.J.Chikokota of the Anglican Church and Rev. Michael John Kajawa of CCAP Nkhoma Synod to Nigeria. They, in-fact had gone for a six weeks intensive course in Christian-Muslim Relations at I badan University.[62]

---

[59] PROCMURA, Theme: Witnessing in Religious Pluralistic Landscape in Africa,Strategic Plan 2007/8 – 2011/12 p.6
[60] .Ibid
[61] .Christian Council of Malawi –AGM- Minutes 6-8 May, 1967.
[62] .Christian Council of Malawi – AGM – Minutes- 8-9,November,1967

During the annual meeting of 4th to 5th May 1971 the General Adviser of IAP Rev. James Crosssley, residing in Nigeria addressed the council in the presence of the three graduates. The Council endorsed, to form an Area Committee straight away. The following were elected into office: -

Rev. Fr. V.B. Chipenda-Chairperson.-Anglican
Rev. M.J.Kajawa. CCAP Nkhoma Synod.
Rev. Fr. A. Lunda, - Anglican
,,   ,,   Chisulu.- Anglican
,,   ,,   Mataka.- Anglican
,,   ,,   Banda. - Anglican and
Rev. John Hill.- Nkhoma Synod. [63]

After the three had reported to the council of their training in Nigeria the Council saw an urgent need for an Area Adviser in the near future for smooth running of the committee.

Since then, General Advisers either called some church leaders for training in Kenya or attended some courses organized by the Area Committee in Malawi e.g. Rev. James Ritchie with Area Adviser of Ethiopia Rev. Dr. Gunner Hassel visited Malawi in 1970 with Rev. TA Beetham- (Associate General Adviser).

Further, in 1975 the Christian council of Malawi also sent late Rev. I.S.Salimoni and Mr. Ernest Mussa of Nkhotakota to undergo six-week intensive course in Nairobi Kenya in anticipation that Mussa would become an Area Adviser for Islam Africa Project in Malawi.

Subsequently, Rev. late D.P.Gareta represented the council at another meeting about Islam and Christian Muslim Relations in Ghana. This was reported to the council. And it was of paramount importance because the committee upon hearing these reports it got very vibrant in conducting courses in places like along the lakeshore in the areas of Nkhotakota, Salima down to Mangochi,

---

[63] .Christian Council of Malawi- AGM-Minutes No 971, 4-5 November, 1969.

Machinga (Kasupe), Zomba, and as far as Mulanje with church leaders and sometimes the laity.

On other occasions church leaders or Christians were invited to attend such courses at Chilema Church Lay Training Centre or at Chongoni Church Lay Training Center though few people could attend.. [64]

After the expiring period of the existing committee; a new committee was instituted in 1978 at a meeting held at Chilema Church Lay Training Center on 20th January where the following were elected

Rev. M.J.Kajawa-Chairperson.-Nkhoma Synod
Rev. Fr. J.A.Lunda- Recording Secretary.-Anglican
Rev. Fr. V.B. Chipenda.   -Anglican
Rev. J.L.M. Kapolo,   -Blantyre Synod
,, D.P.Gareta.   – Nkhoma Synod
,, I.S.Salimoni.   – Nkhoma Synod
,, G.A.Kachaje.   – Nkhoma Synod
,, R.G. Masamba.   - Blantyre Synod
Fr. G.A.Mchekama.   - Anglican.

After, reflecting of late Rev. D.P.Gareta's report of his attendance of a meeting in Accra on Christian Muslim Relations. The committee recommended the former for further studies at a more advanced degree level or above in anticipation for him to become the Area Adviser for Malawi Area Committee. [65]

Therefore, the Council that met from 2nd to 3rd May 1978 endorsed Gareta's name for a three-year course degree programme at Beruit University. This materialized. After, Beirut he went to Fuller Theological Seminary for his masters. Upon completion of his training returned home but his mission was cut short by his sudden death, a car accident when returning from a Synod meeting. What a shock! For Malawi area committee.

---

[64] Christian Council of Malawi – AGM-Minutes No71/39 – 4-5 May, 1971.
[65] Christian Council of Malawi – AGM – Minutes No 71.39. 14 November,1971

But the Malawi area committee then sent late Rev. Ted Mwambila of the Livingstonia Synod, late Fr. E.E.Malunda and the author to Selly Oak Colleges in Birmingham in the United Kingdom for training in Christian Muslim Relations on different occasions respectively. They all graduated with certificate, Diploma and Postgraduate Diploma respectively. Then late Fr. E.E.Malunda was appointed Area Adviser in 2002 but passed away in short while late Rev. Ted Mwambila was the chairperson of Malawi area committee while the author is now the current Area Adviser since 2003.[66]

Further, the author has made an extensive research of the impact PROCMURA has made by looking at the areas late Rev. M.J.Kajawa pastored, for his research for Masters Degree with the University of Malawi. The present Area - committee, which is rather so called dormant due to lack of funding in the few past years, had the following members from member churches.

Late Rev. Ted Mwambila - Chairperson.-Livingstonia Synod.
Late Rev. Fr. Ndomondo –Anglican.
Rev. D.R.Mtipela   -Blantyre Synod retired
Rev.M.J.Sande   Blantyre Synod
Fr. Anderson L.Kasiya. -Anglican
Rev. Butawo –Baptist.
   ,,   Muwalo -Baptist
Rev. Mabuwa Baptist and Rev A.J.M. Mnthambala as Area Adviver of Malawi PROCMURA Area Committee.[67]

Area committee activities

Almost all the early instituted Area Committees were so vibrant conducting courses for church leaders or Christians or Christians and Muslims together. This was carried out at area level in the respective places by inviting participants for residential training in

---

[66] Christian Council of Malawi –AGM – Minutes 2 – 3 May, 1978.

[67] The Area committee has been somehow dormant after the pass on of Rev.Ted Mwambila awaiting for institution of a new committee. One thing operational is that the Area Adviser is a lecturer at Zomba Theological College and teaches Islam/Christian Muslim Relations.

lay training centers like Nkhotakota or Chongoni in the central region or Chilema Lay Training centre in the Southern region. The meetings ranged from one, three, five day Seminars or workshops.

The curriculum included

1. Constitution and Objectives of Islam Africa Project (now - PROCMURA).

Islam and its history.
History of Islam in Africa.
History of Islam in Malawi
The Quran.
The Quranic Interpretation
The way of worship.

Sufism and Muslim-Brotherhoods

Christian Interpretation in the Muslim world.
The Hadith.

History of Christian Muslim Relations

Issues in Christian Muslim Relations.
Witness and Dialogue.
    This work is carried out by the Malawi Council of Churches then Christian Council of Malawi which is the grouping of protestant churches in Malawi.[68]

The Malawi Area committee challenges and way forward

The impact

The history of PROCMURA in Malawi has been strong all through by conducting various courses such as: - Church leaders, women, and

---

[68] See the appendix for the full list of the member churches of the Malawi Council of Churches then Christian Council of Malawi

the youth. The effect this has made is worth mentioning, for example the area that late Rev. M.J.Kajawa served most congregations' reveal a taste of PROCMURA's approach. This has been proved by the author while researching for his Masters Degree with the University of Malawi.

What has been discovered is that there is good and strong relationship among Muslims and Christian's evident at grassroots level. If ever conflict occurs it is sporadic experience and usually caused by foreign influences and unthinkable for the indigenous population.

Other babies born out of the influence of Procmura's work in Malawi may include

Public Affairs Committee (PAC)

Is a committee formed between 1990 and 1991. A grouping that comprises Malawi Council Member churches, the Episcopal Conference of Malawi (Roman Catholics), Qadria-Muslim Association of Malawi (QMAM) and Muslim Association of Malawi (MAM) and other stakeholders that helped peaceful transition from one party system of government to multi-party democracy and later other agencies were incorporated into the grouping. The grouping is operational to this day as a watch dog on the government policies in its affairs in the running of the government in matters.

Malawi Interfaith Aids Association (MIAA)

The following grouping after PAC is Malawi Interfaith Aids Association (MIAA) whose objective is to answer the question of how the inter-faith community can team up to fight against the pandemic of HIV and AIDS. This grouping has the following members - Malawi Council of Churches, Episcopal Conference of Malawi (Catholics), and Evangelical Association of Malawi, Qadria-Muslim Association of Malawi (QMAM) and Muslim Association of Malawi (MAM) and other stakeholders. It teams up the faith communities to fight against Aids pandemic on the cross boarder of faith.

The teaching of Islam in high learning institutions is available i.e. The University of Malawi, Theological institutions. What remains is the introduction of the teaching of Christian Muslim Relations proper as a subject.

The most inter-faith dialogue takes place at grass root level for example at markets, funerals, weddings, political party gatherings. etc.

The way forward

The great need for sustainability of PROCMURA's programme is training more church leaders, women leaders and youth leaders in the awareness of inter-faith dialogue i.e. Muslims or Christians are our permanent neighbours therefore they must know each other. The introduction of Christian – Muslim Relations as a subject alongside Islam is of paramount importance in all institutions of high learning.

For that to take place sensitization of institutions throughout the country on Christian Muslim Relations awareness is vital. This could obviously bring in more understanding between Muslims and Christians and so living in diversity in peace would be a possible solution

Furthermore, the women's programmes would bring an understanding of team work to Muslim and Christian women under PROCMURA to work together to combat HIV and AIDS, empowering women and the youth on issues of poverty and how to look after orphans. Before, seeking help from outside world as faith communities to set a good example.

Conclusion

So far so good that Christians and Muslims are permanent neighbours, what remains is to sustain and maintain the good neighbourliness; to accept one another regardless of faith, colour, or ethnic grouping within our vicinity. PROCMURA's approach of interpreting the Gospel of Jesus Christ faithfully and responsibly in the Muslim world stands out as of parmount importance for the issue of conversion is the duty of the Holy Spirit or of almighty God and not human activity.

Secondly, Christians and Muslims are to engage in constructive dialogue for peaceful co-existence in diversity. Here, we would like to see a Christian or a Muslim prove of their religion in the way they testify through their life style as a living testimony as we live side by side

Chapter Three

Interfaith dialogue in CCAP Nkhoma Synod, 1889–2007

The road that Nkhoma Synod has traveled in the mission field towards Muslims reminds us of the English proverb which says, "History is the best teacher." That is to say, you cannot go forward in life, into the future, without the knowledge of the past. The past always determines the road of the future. For example, two years ago you may have missed a mark in life; you would therefore tend to avoid repeating the same thing. Chris Blignaut in the Nkhoma Synod CCAP museum brochure writes,

> "Life is lived by looking forward, but understood by looking backward."[69]

The journey was begun by two people, namely Revs Andrew Charles Murray and T.C.B. Vlok. They pitched a tent at Katawa near Chief Chiwere's headquarters on 28th November 1889. They faced total heathendom in the form of African Traditional Religion, plus absolute illiteracy.[70] There at Katawa they dedicated themselves to God for the duty to founding a church based on the Word of God. Their emphasis was on the Biblical message of salvation of man from sin through Jesus Christ. They intended to establish a church that would become a self-governing, self-propagating and self-supporting church in this part of the world.

They immediately started schools nearly in all surrounding villages. They wanted followers of Christ to learn how to read and write, before they could receive baptism. Therefore, a few people were trained as teacher-evangelists and those who became teacher-evangelists played a significant role in spreading the Gospel. They were called monitors. They produced a church well

---

[69] Chris Blignaut, in *Nkhoma Synod CCAP. Museum brochure*, p. 1.
[70] Martin C. Pauw, *Mission and Church in Malawi: The History of Nkhoma Synod of the Church of Central Africa Presbyterian 1889-1962*, p. 5.

versed in the scriptures.[71] The first converts were baptized in 1895 at Mvera and by 1900 small Christian communities existed at Mvera (151 communicant members), Malembo (85), Kongwe (32), Nkhoma (31) and Livulezi (92).[72]

Soon the need arose for the formation of a 'Council of Congregations' in the year 1903. The council had representation of the few congregations already established which functioned as a Presbytery. Later, the Presbytery grew and became a Synod which later joined the other two Presbyteries of Livingstonia and Blantyre to form what is now known as Church of Central Africa Presbyterian in 1926 after two years of observation since its establishment in 1924. This body which was known as CCAP General Synod is now called CCAP General Assembly.[73] The work has progressed well to this day. The emphasis of mission to Muslims today is along the lakeshore, covering the districts of Nkhotakota, Salima, part of Dedza, part of Ntcheu and part of Mangochi. The work is renamed 'Neighbour Mission' as mandated by the Synod of Nkhoma CCAP constitution on Mission to Muslims. The other three arms of the Mission Department, apart from Neighbour Mission, include home mission, Mphatso Synod in Mozambique, and South Africa.

3.2 New wave to missions

It was noted from the beginning that another challenge ahead was the work among the Muslims, most of them of the Yao tribe.[74] This marked the beginning of Christian – Muslim relations in the CCAP Nkhoma Synod though with an antagonistic mindset' which has gradually changed to the moderate approach of dialogue.[75]

---

[71] Ibid. p. 6.
[72] Martin C. Pauw, *Mission and Church in Malawi: The History of Nkhoma Synod of the Church of Central Africa Presbyterian 1889-1962*, p. 6.
[73] Livingstonia and Blantyre had formed the CCAP in 1924, Nkhoma joined in 1926.
[74] Martin C Pauw, *Mission and Church in Malawi: The History of Nkhoma Synod of the Church of Central Africa Presbyterian 1889-1962*, p. 95.
[75] Ibid.

One historical aspect to note is that there were many Muslims along the lakeshore, with centres in Nkhotakota and in the upland region on the highlands of Chitundu and south-westward plains of Dedza district. The Yao of the upland region of Mayani area were under Chief Tambala, also known as Chitundu. There had been contacts between Nkhotakota and Tambala since 1891.[76] While doing their work of missions among those who followed the African Traditional Religion, the question arose among the DRC missionaries, "how do we spread the Gospel among these Muslims in this area?"[77]

To answer this question, Rev A.L. Hofmeyer was asked to do research about the Muslim influence in Nyasaland, in particular in the Central Province now Central Region. The Dutch Reformed Church in South Africa was very anxious of the situation of Muslims in their mission area. Therefore, A.L. Hofmeyer embarked on the research by visiting Nkhotakota, Salima, the area around Nkhoma station in particular, the eastern part called Chitundu and as far as Zomba among the Yao, where Islam seemed taking ground. In his findings, he estimated 150,000 Muslims in the whole of Nyasaland.

3.2.1 Rev A.L. Hofmeyr's findings

He discovered that Islam was alive among the Yao, and the inhabitants had influence in the community of Nkhotakota where Muslims were mostly found and that they did not allow the missionaries to open schools in their respective villages. However, the mission schools in the Muslim villages were declining except those amongst the Nyanja villages, which were flourishing. The Muslims' desire was to let their children learn Arabic and the Quran, their Holy Book. Each village had its own *mwalimu* (teacher) with influence in the community whom the village-headmen relied upon as advisors. In addition, he saw that Muslims were really utilizing Fridays for *Ijumaa* prayers as their Sunday.

---

[76] Ibid. p. 95.
[77] Nkhoma Synod, Zolamulira (Constitution), (1932, 54), 1970, p. 79.

3.2.2 His recommendations

After evaluation of his findings he made the following recommendations: That mission stations should be erected wherever possible and that men be appointed for the purpose of working amongst the Muslims as evangelists. They should be Yao teachers who would teach in the Yao language and not in Chinyanja. Further, the workers should undergo training to learn Arabic so that they would be able to read the Quran. For example the story of Mary, the mother of Jesus, and the virgin birth are mentioned in the Quran (Sura 19:19-21).

This would therefore enable such evangelists to utilize their knowledge of Arabic in sharing Jesus Christ with Muslims by making references to what the Quran says about the two. He ended his report by challenging the Dutch Reformed Church in South Africa to act promptly by doing something to the glory of God in this regard.

The Council of Congregations heard the report of his research in 1909. By then, there were already distinct areas where a population of thirty to forty thousand Muslims lived. Such areas having major Muslim population were as follows (1) Malembo district (the Phirilongwe) (2) Mvera district (lakeshore around Salima) (3) Nkhoma district (Tambala's land) and (4) Chinthembwe, (Ntchisi district – Jumbe's people around Nkhotakota).[78] The report of A.L. Hofmeyer emphasized the establishment of congregations, the personnel development in such fields and to undergo training in Islamic studies first in order to be equipped for the ministry.

But the work was slowed down with the outbreak of sleeping sickness and the First World War in 1914. By then the missionaries had already divided the Muslim mission area into two parts called

---

[78] A.L. Hofmeyr, "Islam in Nyasaland" (1910), in David S. Bone (ed.), *Malawi's Muslims: Historical Perspectives: Islam in Nyasaland*, Blantyre: CLAIM-Kachere, 2000, pp. 165-172; Martin C. Pauw, *Mission and Church in Malawi: The History of Nkhoma Synod of the Church of Central Africa Presbyterian 1889-1962*, p. 95. Ntchisi district comprised Ntchisi of today and the whole of Nkhotakota as one district.

'zones'. These were (i) the whole area along the lakeshore i.e. from Nkhotakota down to Mangochi, called the Lakeshore Zone. (ii) The Upland Zone that comprised Chitundu (Mayani) under chief Tambala, south-westwards to T.A. Kaphuka, T.A. Kachere, and T.A. Mazengera east of Lilongwe. It is the area of Dedza North-West and Lilongwe east, the Nkhoma mission area.

The reality came about in the year 1920 when Rev M.G. Uys was set aside to start work in Tambala's area. This resulted in the opening of Chitundu mission station on 2.8.1923 with schools around already in operation. M.G. Uys worked in the area for six years until he left the country in 1926.[79] He was replaced by Rev A.G. van Wyk upon returning from his training in Islamic studies in Egypt in the year 1926 to continue the work. A congregation bearing the name Chitundu was established on 30th September 1939 with 426 members and not many were converted Muslims. The Muslim field of evangelism proved the most difficult one to handle. Van Wyk had to leave the country the following year.[80]

The departure of van Wyk led to the rise of 'Malawi missionaries'. One may ask what the term 'Malawi missionaries' means? A Malawi missionary in this context is the one who adheres to the Great Commission of Jesus Christ (Matthew 28:19-20) regardless of colour or ethnic grouping or where the work is undertaken. When we talk of Malawi missionaries we refer to the Malawians involved in the field of spreading the Good News of Jesus Christ to various parts, whether in Malawi or outside; but in this context we are talking of missionaries towards the Muslims. Though Nkhoma Synod was busy making strategies for missions to Muslims, she was also busy sending Malawi missionaries to Zambia, Zimbabwe, and even to South Africa and Mozambique where the mission work is expanding to this day.

---

[79] Martin C. Pauw, *Mission and Church: The History of Nkhoma Synod of the Church of Central Africa Presbyterian 1889-1962*, p. 95.
[80] Ibid. p. 95.

Thus, late John Michael Kajawa, a Malawian, followed after the departure of M.G. Uys and A.G. van Wyk respectively.[81] John M. Kajawa was born in 1922 to a family of five children, two boys and three girls. His father Fletcher Kajawa came from Naisi village, T/A Malemia – Zomba and was a Yao and his mother Che Fulose, a Muslim from Susa village, T/A Malemia, Domasi and his mother was later converted to Christianity.

John Michael Kajawa married Nelly Kajawa in 1935 whose wedding ceremony took place at Zomba CCAP. His wife Nelly came from Chiwaka Village, T/A Mazengera (Nkhoma mission area), Lilongwe. They were blessed with eleven children.

Upon joining the holy ministry, Kajawa served at Monekera and Chawa (1963-68) and Nkhotakota (1968-73). He went to work at Chitundu (1973-76), Dedza Boma (1980-88) and Mthandiza (1988-96), and Mndolera congregations respectively and retired from the holy ministry in 1997. He passed on to live with the Lord in 2004.

His wife Nelly, has also passed on but she lived exemplary life, assisting her husband with her fluent Yao accent. Though a Chewa by tribe and background, made headway in the ministry with her husband. This was a great asset for this family in the holy ministry among Muslims. Among the congregations that he served, only Mlanda (1976-80) and Mndolera (1996-97) have sporadic numbers of Muslim communities.

His services at Nkhotakota were interrupted with the offer of a scholarship by PROCMURA in 1971 through the Malawi Council of Churches (then Christian Council of Malawi). Therefore he went to Ibadan University in Nigeria for one academic year for a course on how to share Christ with Muslims. He graduated with a certificate in Christian – Muslim Relations.

After a car accident on Salima road D.P. Gareta lost his life. Then, Rev John Michael Kajawa became an Interim Area Advisor in his place for Malawi under the Christian Council of Malawi. It was at the same period that the council was looking for someone to fill the

---

[81] Nkhoma Synod CCAP, *Zolamulira (Constitution)*, Nkhoma Press, 1970 p. 79.

gap. This made Nkhoma Synod send the author to South Africa at Rand Afrikaans University in 1993 under the sponsorship of the Synod and later to Selly Oak Colleges, Birmingham University in the United Kingdom for Islamic Studies in the academic year 1997/98 under PROCMURA sponsorship through the Malawi Council of Churches.

Kajawa's friend Michael Z. Khombe testifies that Kajawa's favourite sermon was from the Gospel of John 12:21 with the theme "I want to see Jesus. We want to see Jesus." John. Michael Kajawa also wrote two books on how to relate to Muslim neighbours. (i) *Nkhosa Yosokera* (The Lost Sheep) and *Chenjezo la Mulungu kwa Anthu Ake* (God's Warning to his People). He too participated in the translation of the book entitled *Al-Kitab* (The Book) from English into Chichewa with Rev G.A. Kachaje . The book assists Muslims to understand essential issues about Christianity but also assists Christians on how to help Muslims understand more about Christianity.

Kajawa had the opportunity to practice the techniques and skills that he acquired in Nigeria in the congregations he served in his lifetime. The area researched is the area M.J. Kajawa, a proponent of PROCMURA, had ministered and probably his experience in Christian – Muslim relations in this area had influence and impact upon the people. This includes all congregations except Nkhoma, Chimbiya, Mphunzi and Mtenthera in the Upland Zone.

Kajawa was succeeded by D.P. Gareta in 1973, at Nkhotakota congregation, where it did not take long for him to secure a scholarship for Islamic Studies in Kenya and the United States of America. Unfortunately he passed on in a car accident upon his return to Malawi.

3.3 Fruits of mission to Muslims

Though it seems that most conversions must have resulted from antagonistic approach and none from the PROCMURA approach, there could not be a total demarcation between the two but the fact is that both approaches were applied at one time or another and so had some influence and results that the Synod is enjoying today.

Other benefits for Nkhoma Synod CCAP that need a mention include the conversion of some Muslims at Chitundu in Tambala's area in the Upland Zone. One converted Muslim, James Kathumba, became a teacher and was later called by the Lord to the holy ministry and then became a minister of the word and sacrament.

The mission work of the DRC, both in general and to Muslims in particular, resulted in the establishment of congregations of the CCAP Nkhoma Synod i.e. Nkhoma (1896), Mphunzi (1912), Chawa (1963), Monekera (1963), Chitundu (1922), Mthandiza (1958), Mtenthera (1971), Madalitso (2000), Chimbiya (2003) and Makungubwi (2005) congregations, with so many prayer houses in the respective congregations in Muslim communities of the Upland Zone.

James Kathumba served at his home congregation Chitundu CCAP, and later served at Monekera, now Madalitso congregation. Being of a Muslim background, he was not denied to wear his cap in church. That principle applied also to other Muslim converts. Another convert was Rev Sendera from a Muslim village called Thyola Khosi in Chawa CCAP congregation. He too served at Chitundu CCAP and later went to work at Chikoma CCAP congregation.

The third known Muslim convert to put on record is M.J. Kajawa as mentioned earlier, originally from Zomba born to a Muslim mother and Christian father. He served in the Synod of Nkhoma extensively on mission to Muslims.[82] The newly ordained minister Rev D.T.A. Juma was born of a Yao Muslim father from Tambala area in Chitundu congregation and of a Christian Ngoni mother. He served at Thawale, Youth Department, Chikuluti congregations and is now at Kasemba congregation in the city of Lilongwe to this day. All the above examples are from the Upland Zone except Kajawa.

---

[82] Christian Council of Malawi, Council minutes, 1972.

The above list emphasizes the concept of Malawi missionaries who have actually come from the Islamic background in serving the Lord.

Along the Lakeshore Zone the birth of so many congregations in the Muslim areas from Nkhotakota down to Mangochi is evident in the establishment of such congregations, with numerous prayer houses i.e. congregation of Nkhotakota (1967 as a congregation), Kolowiro (a station in 1914 and a congregation in 1946). Matenje became a station in 1915 and a congregation in 1955, Thavite, previously known as Matombozi, became a congregation in 1995.

In addition Msenjere congregation was born in 1999, while Mpatsa became a congregation in 1946 and Msalura a prayer house to Mpatsa was set aside as a congregation in 1990. The congregation of Malowa was established in 1976. All the above congregations are found in Salima district except Msenjere and Nkhotakota which are in Nkhotakota district. If you go further south we have Monkey Bay congregation born in 1990 while the mother church Malembo CCAP (a station on 24th July 1904 but a congregation in 1909) with so many prayer houses some of which are already upgraded to congregation status for example Monkey Bay CCAP congregation. Other old congregations established along the lakeshore include Khola congregation in the year 1918 and Mtakataka in 1948.

It is interesting that, though the missionaries noted that evangelism among Muslims was difficult and had to be performed without immediate results, success has to be highlighted from the ministry of Kajawa at Nkhotakota, as he had 100 converts, in a congregation where he found 40 members he left 451 communicant members, Muslims inclusive, 365 catechumen members, Muslims inclusive, he found two prayer houses but left 7 prayer houses within the Muslim villages. The statistics of Muslim coverts to Christianity increased which the Lord provided each day.

Further, at Chitundu another convert that needs a mention is village headman Tawe. By the time of interview he was an elder representing the session among the women's guild members in the congregation. Sheiks Adule and Chikonde are now members of the church at Chitundu.

As from the Neighbour Mission report the recent situation in the years of 2000 to 2006, establishment of the Mission Department has enabled a substantial increase of converts as has been observed in most of the congregations along the lakeshore with a remarkable achievement. In the congregations of Malowa there were thirteen of them in 2005 and nine converts in 2006 and among them we have Akimu, Sumani, Yusufu, Swaleyi to mention a few. In the same period Mtakataka had two neighbours that received the grace of God through Jesus Christ. The congregation of Msalura during the period 2001 to 2003 had fourteen converts e.g. Patuma, Waziri, Salida, Dunia, Mariam, Masistala as new members of the congregation. In the congregation of Nkhotakota in the same period fifteen conversions were experienced and new brothers and sisters in the Lord were added, some of whom were Asile, Mandaaliza, Adijah, Marita, Daina to mention a few and this continues each day as the years go by.

3.3.1 Mission structures.

Despite hiccups experienced by the CCAP Synod of Nkhoma in the field of mission to Muslims, some achievements have materialized at institutional level. One of such is the Mission Department with three aspects: (1) Mission to Muslims in Malawi and (2) foreign missions to Portuguese East Africa (Mphatso Synod) and (3) home mission in which the former is included. The former was renamed 'Neighbour Mission' with concentration along the lakeshore area i.e. from Nkhotakota via Salima to the congregation of Malembo in Mangochi. There is a sub-office in Salima under the Mission Department heading the 'Neighbour Mission'.

In the 1970s the contacts with PROCMURA availed and this led to the involvement of M.J. Kajawa in his training in Christian – Muslim Relations and application of his expertise within the Synod. Further, Rev S.P. Chalera and Rev I.S. Salimoni, both Nkhoma Synod ministers, attended a workshop organized by PROCMURA on 21st

August, 1972. The main speaker at the meeting at Chilema Lay Training Center in Zomba district was Rev Tom Beetham, then General Advisor for PROCMURA. This resulted in the formation of the first area committee under the Christian Council; the first area committee chairperson for Malawi was Rev Fr. B. Malango. He became a Bishop in Zambia and later the Archbishop of Upper Shire and retired from active service in 2007.

Later, late Rev I.S. Salimoni of Nkhoma Synod CCAP attended the Annual General Meeting of PROCMURA held in Nairobi, Kenya in 1989 as a representative of the Malawi Council of Churches where he was elected member of the executive committee, a post he held until 1992. He was replaced by late Rev Ted Mwambila. He was a minister of Livingstonia Synod CCAP, and served as Area Committee chairperson of Malawi under the Malawi Council of Churches. Rev.I.S.Salimoni has since passed on in January,2020.

3.4 Salvation outside the visible – church

Although the 'Neighbour Mission' work is taking roots in Nkhoma Synod CCAP, there is one important issue to clarify concerning mission work among Muslims. That fundamental question is, "Is there salvation outside the visible church of Christ?"[83]

The term 'visible church' in this context refers to the Christian fellowship that gathers to worship the almighty God through Jesus Christ. In Reformed Theology, there is the differentiation of special grace operative in the order of salvation and of universal grace in the order of creation. A deeper understanding of universal grace would prompt us to embark on dialogue because we would see the providence of God in the other faiths. This would help us have a sympathetic and loving attitude to move forward with more understanding in the field of missions. The term love in this context refers to that love of God for his creation, in particular, mankind.[84]

---

[83] Patrick A. Kalilombe, *Doing Theology at the Grassroots. Theological Essays from Malawi,* Gweru: Mambo-Kachere, 1999, p. 106.
[84] John 3:16.

With regard to the Roman Catholic Church's teaching, the Vatican II Council opens a way. Patrick Kalilombe writes,

> "Those also can attain everlasting salvation who through no fault of their own do not know the Gospel of Christ or His church, yet sincerely seek God and, moved by grace, strive by their deeds to do His will as it is known to them through the dictates of conscience."[85]

In this respect, there is still room for the Synod of Nkhoma to investigate and do more research on the question in relation to Calvinistic theology as understood by Reformed theology, whether there could be elements of salvation in those religions pointing to Jesus. Therefore, the next question is simply, what is the position of Nkhoma Synod regarding salvation of people of other faith communities against the antagonistic approach as if they were empty slates?

Perhaps Ecumenical theology or Orthodox theology can be of help as a guiding factor in comparing with the view of the Second Vatican Council.

For example the Africans born before the coming of Christianity did not choose to be born in Africa without the knowledge of Jesus Christ. Further, among them were those whose morality was good in the sight of mankind until their death. They are the ones called the living-dead among Africans because their example still speaks to the living today. Are we correct to say that all born before Jesus are damned for hell? Or are we to take the view of Peter that when Christ descended into hell he preached to those in prison?[86] Reformed Theology knows of universal grace, and this could be enriched by the concept of special grace of God.[87]

---

[85] Patrick A. Kalilombe, *Doing Theology at the Grassroots. Theological Essays from Malawi*, Gweru: Mambo-Kachere, 1999, p. 107.
[86] 1 Peter 3:19.
[87] Anthony M. Coniaris, *The Orthodox Church. Its Faith and Life*, Minneapolis: Light and Life Publishing, 1982, pp. 47-55.

Of course, the living dead were not aware of such a grace to embrace it in the presence of the church. In other words, people are sacred even before they come to realize their salvation because of their ignorance of such a grace. Therefore, when we talk of dialogue we must pre-suppose the saving opportunities available before the church for man to acknowledge and accept Jesus as Lord and Saviour. The Orthodox Church teaches that everyone

"was saved on a Friday afternoon at three o'clock in the spring of the year 33 CE, on a hill outside the city of Jerusalem."[88]

This implies that salvation is comprehensive and that it has to do with the past through baptism after an individual accepts Jesus as Lord and Saviour, and this is called *'justification'*. Then, what follows thereafter is that we are continually being saved daily as we walk and grow into adulthood in life with Christ and the Holy Spirit, and this is known as *'sanctification'*. The last phase is the future of our final glory in Christ called *'glorification* in eternity'.[89]

In other words, salvific activity is a process that started in eternity and continues until Christ comes in His glory as King into eternity. That is why Orthodox theology holds that salvation is not static but dynamic towards receiving the fullness of God's life, and that it can never be achieved fully in this life.[90] But the essence of it is the receiving part through faith. That means it is through the process that the true essence of salvation is attained regardless of the religion one belonged to at first, but once an individual accepted Jesus as personal saviour, that will help him to transform to the Glory of God as the receiving part of this salvation.

3.4.1 Nkhoma's approach

The next question to ask is; how does Nkhoma Synod proceed in mission work among people of other faiths communities, in particular Muslims? When the first missionaries came, their

---

[88] Ibid. p. 50.
[89] Colossians 3:4 (RSV).
[90] Anthony M. Coniaris, *The Orthodox Church. Its Faith and Life*, Minneapolis: Light and Life Publishing:, 1982, pp. 47-55.

teaching emphasized conversion with very little or no dialogue at all, overlooking God's ability of salvific activity outside the Christian Church.[91]

Later, the Synod embraced PROCMURA's approach which may seem to contradict the Reformed tradition based on Calvinistic theology. This demands further research and investigation as the Synod embarks on inter-faith dialogue with Muslims as neighbours. That is why the question of mission to Muslims remains a challenge till today because the Synod realizes that Muslims are our *'permanent'* neighbours and are here to stay.[92] Kaufa writes,

> Muslims are everywhere in the country so that it would be absurd to attempt to marginalize them once again. The beautiful mosques and *madras* (schools) built within the last decade prove that Islam has really come to stay.[9]

That being the case, it is high time to promote good neighbourly relations to undo the antagonistic missionary approach. The missionary approach always produced a stormy and tense atmosphere between Muslims and Christians. For example, the preaching by some Nkhoma missionaries in 1953 at Linthipe, which was against Muslims, aroused commotion; though diversity in methods of approach may still exist. In order to move forward in the mission field, in particular with Christian – Muslim relations, the Synod has now established a Mission Department with a section responsible for mission to Muslims, with its own terms of reference and procedures as a guide for proper conduct of the work among people of other faith communities.

The expression "Neighbour Mission" is a new term in the Synod of Nkhoma for evangelism among Muslims to effect the present day expression of Christian – Muslim relations. It is an attitude

---

[91] Patrick A. Kalilombe, *Doing Theology at the Grass-roots. Theological Essays from Malawi,* Gweru: Mambo-Kachere, 1999, p. 107.
[92] David S. Bone (ed.), *Malawi's Muslim. Historical Perspectives*, p. 14. Andrew U. Kaufa, Muslim – Christian Dialogue: A Challenge to Christian Churches in Malawi, unpublished, p. 9. .

embraced by the church as early as the 1970s.[93] The mission department was put in place in 1977 and Ryk van Velden became the first mission secretary.

As an area of interest the Synod needs continuity in the field of missions to Muslims whose work re-started on 22.2.1999 with a committee instituted at a meeting held at Msalura CCAP congregation in Salima Township under the Neighbour Mission. At this meeting members were incorporated into the committee as follows:- Mr. Ndalama of Chipoka Secondary School in Malowa Congregation and Ms. Laubscher of Nkhoma hospital, a member of Nkhoma Congregation. But elections of office bearers were postponed to a later date.

3.5 Neighbour mission

The work began as early as the 1930s, while Nkhoma was still a presbytery in the two distinctive areas called zones:-

(a) The Islamic zone of the lakeshore area.
(b) The Islamic zone of the upland region around Chitundu.[94]

The Neighbour Mission's work has shifted direction from Chitundu towards the lakeshore area in the districts of Nkhotakota, Salima, Dedza, Ntcheu and part of Mangochi, respectively. This does not imply neglecting other areas in the Synod.

The Neighbour Mission has now an office with a coordinator in Salima Township. The post of the coordinator was at first a temporary one but has now become a full-time post with three resource persons from every five congregations and two full senior and eight junior staff members. The Neighbour Mission committee saw the need to have a 'policy' to guide the performance of the work. A task force was appointed to put in place such a policy. After all drafts of the said documents had been scrutinized, the committee presented its findings before the main Mission Committee.

---

[93] Nkhoma Synod, Synod Minutes, S3332, 1993.
[94] John 1:1-4 (RSV).

After thorough discussions and adjustments the matter was referred to Synod by the main mission committee at its assembly held 18-25 October, 1999 at Namon Katengeza Church Lay Training Center where the Synod of Nkhoma approved and endorsed the policy to be a proper document to guide the work among Muslims.[95]

3.5.1 Principles for Christian – Muslim relations in the neighbour mission

In the policy of how to share Christ with our neighbours a few things may be highlighted as main stepping stones. This policy covers such issues as broad objectives, respect and love towards Muslims. The mandate to know them through study of their religion is obviously imperative for those who work in the field.

3.5.2 Broad objectives

The Synod shall embark on mobilizing its members to love and respect Muslims and witness for Christ by making disciples among them. This shall allow members to understand the Muslim neighbour and his religion and encourage the Christian youth to stand firm in their Christian faith as they share the Gospel with their Muslim counterparts to the glory of God.

3.5.3 Respect and love as imperative towards our Muslim Neighbours.

Nkhoma Synod shall make every effort to encourage its members to love and respect the Muslim neighbour and appreciate the fellowship there upon. The view of Muslims as enemies shall be opposed at any cost.

3.5.4 Knowledge increase and understanding of Muslim Neighbour

Nkhoma Synod shall encourage its members to understand the Muslim and his religion through seminars, literature distribution and correspondence courses for easy sharing of Christ.

---

[95] Synod Minutes number 3332: c,d, p. 9.

3.5.5 Stand firm in faith

Nkhoma Synod shall assist its members to stand firm in their faith, in particular its youth and new converts and make them ready for any spiritual war that the devil may bring over them.

3.5.6 Training and discipleship.

Nkhoma Synod shall train resource persons at every level that is Congregation, Presbytery and Synod levels, and make disciples all those that come before Jesus and help them grow in faith and be ready to share the Gospel.

3.5.7 Care for newly borns

Nkhoma Synod shall take responsibility by encouraging its members to both have an open mind and to welcome the newly borns in their respective homes. Further, promote special funding for care and introduction of literacy classes for those who may need them.

3.5.8 Structure and policies

Nkhoma Synod shall embark on love expression and unity among believers for faithful and responsible witnessing and discipleship for Christ at all levels.

3.5.9 Promotion of good relations and dialogue with our neighbours

Nkhoma Synod shall encourage her church leaders and believers to establish a table for dialogue on issues of the interfaith community, and settle any disputes as early as possible at the local level. Further, to encourage church leaders to work ecumenically with other churches/government for settling any conflicts that may arise.

3.5.10 Policy highlights.

When you read the policy you will discover that it is rich in its contents and good for the spread of the Gospel. If you read closely point no. 2 entitled "The Promotion of Respect and Love for Muslims," sub-topic 2.1 says:-

> "Special efforts to be made to encourage Christians to love their Muslim neighbours and bestow respect, help and appreciation for them. The attitude to view Muslims as enemies will be opposed" (see also 9).[96]

This reveals, to the reader; that the *'love'* the Synod expresses towards the Gospel for Muslim neighbours is great. On the one hand there is a total denial of violence, antagonism, or an absurd or negative approach in sharing Jesus and his salvation to mankind. On the other hand, if you read point four ("The protection of Christianity against Islam"), in particular 4.3, it seems different:

> "Nkhoma Synod to encourage ecumenical bodies to which it belongs, for example, the Malawi Council of Churches or the Evangelical Association of Malawi to mention a few to speak on behalf of the Christians if it happens that Muslims abuse political, social or economic institutions or organizations to promote Islam in Malawi or to oppose or to attack Christians and the church."[97]

Upon reading these statements one may think that there is contradiction. The latter statement is too strong and apologetic, contrary to the former. In fact, if you read such a statement in isolation, you may encounter such understanding but when you read the policy as a unity, the two statements complement each other for one common good, namely good relationships. The hypothesis in this regard is the desire for good neighbourliness which must be promoted for Malawians because Malawi is our home and it is our responsibility to avoid as much as possible any violence or conflict that would arise from religious fanaticism.

Point 8.2 of the Policy has already started bearing fruit. Point 7 reads: "The Care for Converted Muslims" and sub-topic 8.2 says

---

[96] Nkhoma Synod CCAP, *Synod Mission Policy*, 1999 p. 7.
[97] Ibid. p. 9.

"Congregations to be encouraged to establish a special fund for assistance to converted Muslims and the families who care for them."[98]

There is indeed need for funding and congregations and well-wishers are offering scholarships for secondary education to needy orphans regardless of religion, converted Muslims included. Seven nursery schools have been established in villages in the area to cater for all children regardless of religious affiliations.

Further, the Synod shares her resources with non-Christian communities, in particular Muslims. For example in the field of education the Synod shares her resources with other faith communities such as the primary and secondary schools, some of which are private, Nkhoma College of Nursing to mention a few where it would be possible to close doors to other faith communities. This is true of Nkhoma Hospital where admittance is open to all from around and afar.

3.6 Inter-faith reflections of dialogue.

In summary, some highlights of what Michael John Kajawa accomplished in his ministry on Christian – Muslim relations need a mention. As pastor in all congregations that he served predominantly in Muslim communities his experience and expertise confirms of what transpires today in the social, religious, economic setting of the area under study. Upon interviewing him of what he would say of his success, he emphasized the following three points.

3.6.1 How to approach people of other faiths.

In order to maintain a successful ministry among people of other faith communities, in particular Muslims, he sought first to get to know the people, their background and environment, their needs and their culture before indulging in any form of evangelism. One way of doing it was attending all inter-religious functions such as

---

[98] Ibid.

festivals, funerals or wedding celebrations wherever possible. This, automatically, demands a good relationship between the preacher and the people. That will create a fertile ground for the Gospel in the hearts of the people.

3.6.2 How to preach the word to people of other faiths.[99]

Whenever you preach or share the Gospel, Kajawa said, always preach from the Bible and then compare with the Quran wherever possible in a meaningful way.[100] For example if you preach about the virgin birth of Jesus you would refer to the Quran 19:19 in contrast with the Gospel of Matthew chapter 1:18-25 where this is also mentioned.[101] That is preaching from the known to the unknown. For example a Muslim neighbour believes that Jesus is a prophet but for a Christian Jesus is more than just a prophet but the Son of God.

Further, it is the evangelist's responsibility, after preaching, to wait to hear the feedback; this helps one to improve in the delivering of the Gospel messages in order to touch the hearts of the audience.

3.6.3 Praye.r

When you pay a visit to a Muslim neighbour or family, either in times of joy like marriage ceremonies or in times of crises like funerals or sicknesses, do not rush to pray but always ask for permission to do so. You may never be denied to say a prayer, but it is polite to ask for permission.

3.6.4 Other activities.

Apart from working in various congregations, writing of some books, participating in translation work and even being an Interim Area Advisor for Malawi, he also was involved in conducting seminars within the Synod for both pastors and elders at Namon

---

[99] M.J. Kajawa, *Personal Interview on Christian – Muslim relations*, 08/2003.
[100] M.J. Kajawa, *Personal Interview on Christian – Muslim relations*, 08/2003.
[101] Quran 19:19.

Katengeza Church Lay Training Center. Sometimes he organized such meetings on behalf of Malawi Council of Churches for member churches.

Chapter Four

Living in diversity: a possibility for Christians and Muslims of Dedza North-West and Lilongwe east in peace

4.1 Overview

This chapter describes some aspects of the relationship between Muslims and Christians focusing on Dedza North-West and Lilongwe East, the Nkhoma mission area in the Central Region. It addresses the issue of inter-faith dialogue at grassroots level. In other words, how do Muslims and Christians relate to each other in this area under study? In the survey, different groups were met and interviewed to solicit facts that would reveal the type of relationship existing between them. The two religious communities of Islam and Christianity have a long history in Malawi. Therefore, the ethnic groups in this area include the Chewa, the Yao and the Ngoni. The Asian traders came to the area probably to open businesses. As a result, the Yao who belonged to the Islamic religion carried their religion with them wherever they went and settled. It was only in 1978 when Malawi Congress Party government ordered all Asians to do business in the urban centers and leave the rural areas for the ordinary Malawians to conduct business.

Map of the Area of Study:

Dedza North-West and Nkhoma Mission area (Lilongwe-East).

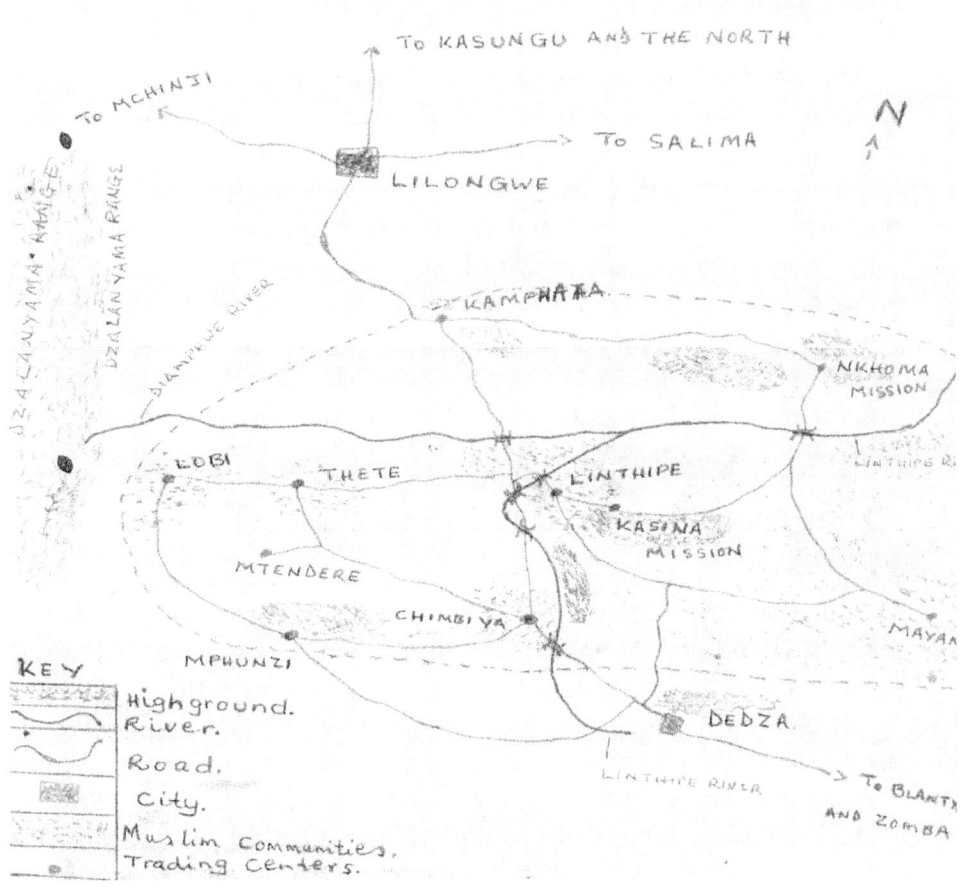

(The sketch of the area of study by the author).

The Nkhoma Synod congregations involved in the research included Chitundu, Makungubwi, Nkhoma, Mthandiza, Madalitso, Monekera, Mphunzi, Chimbiya, Mtenthera and Chawa CCAP while the mosques were Lobi, Thete, Linthipe, Tsoyo, Chimbiya and Mayani respectively. The religious communities, though diverse, interact freely, witnessing for their respective religions. The interest of this book is to concentrate on how Christians and Muslims in this particular area relate to each other. The information gathered was through interviews by personal contact, group and casual meetings or informal discussions wherever possible.

The Muslims interviewed were sheikhs, Muslim men, Muslim women and Muslim youths. The Christians interviewed were church ministers, elders, deacons, youth, women's guild members and ordinary church members. In all cases, they were able to give their own views in regard of the relationship between Muslims and Christians. The issues covered in the questionnaire included knowledge of each other's existence, experiences of conflict, if any, and if not, how peaceful co-existence is maintained in the area. Finally, the book looks at the witnessing for their religions and its impact on both communities and the basis for their unity in the area under study.

4.2 Interfaith dialogue an obligation for Malawi Christians and Muslims

The idea to witness to people of other faiths communities for Christ was the early mandate of the Dutch Reformed Church missionaries.[102] The issue at stake was conversion without dialogue at all. After the work developed, new methods were introduced, especially with the establishment of the Programme for Christian – Muslim Relations in Africa (previously known as Islam Project Africa), which emphasizes dialogue as the ideal way for witnessing

---

[102] Martin Pauw, *History of Nkhoma Synod Church of Central Africa, Presbyterian*, Lusaka: Baptist Press, 1980. p.95.

for Christ among people of other faith communities such as Muslims.

4.2.1. Christians' awareness of Muslims

The question of awareness was looking for information as to when Christians heard of Muslims and what type of relationship exists between them. The respondents to this question were grouped into five categories, each group with its own point of view. The first group of 50% of the Christian respondents stated that they knew of the existence of Muslims since their birth and so had begun relating to them as early as they grew into adulthood.[103] This interaction began when playing together at home in their villages or between their villages or when chasing each other from each other's villages.[104]

The second group of 25% of Christian respondents said that they learnt of Muslims later in life between the 1950s and 1980s respectively.[105] They, perhaps, were born outside the area of study, and only came to the area for work, for example as employees of the government, or for business or marriage or to find settlement. Such circumstances enabled them to relate to Muslims as neighbours, friends, work-mates, partners in business or brothers and sisters, etc.

The third category of 15% of Christian respondents understood the existence of Muslims through attending the same school at primary or secondary level.[106] There are many primary schools in the area. Some of the prominent secondary schools in the area are Mayani, William Murray, Mtendere and Nkhoma, Mkundi, Mayani, Linthipe Community Day Secondary schools to mention a few. In some cases adult literacy programmes run by the government or the Nkhoma Synod's Department of Relief and Development also provided exposure to members of other religious faith groups.

---

[103] Chitundu CCAP views on Christian – Muslim relations, 08/2003.
[104] Chawa CCAP views on Christian – Muslim relations, 08/2003.
[105] Mnthandiza CCAP views on Christian – Muslim relations, 08/2003.
[106] Chitundu CCAP views on Christian – Muslim relations, 08/2003.

The fourth group of 8% of Christian respondents testified that they had knowledge of Muslims through entrepreneurship.[107] Sometimes, some vendors share one bench for selling their commodities at the various markets in the area.

Among the prominent trading centers around this area are: Thete, Mayani, Nkhoma, Linthipe, Chimbiya, Kamphata, Mbuna and Lobi. For example at Lobi trading center a coloured business man, a Muslim, used to shout at non-Muslims who slaughtered goats, cattle or sheep in disregard of Islamic dietary regulations. Asian traders established all markets except Nkhoma, where Asians and missionaries jointly contributed to its establishment.

The last category of 2% of the Christian respondents was not able to specify exactly when they came to know of Muslims in the area. This is probably because they were either not born in the area or came to settle or do business. That being the case they could not know exactly the history of the Muslims. This is true of the movements of most of the Yao Muslims who found settlements in the area of study coming from the lakeshore. This reveals that the Christians have knowledge of the existence of Muslims and that they are able to co-exist peacefully as neighbours, friends, relatives, brothers and sisters, business people and even workmates on a daily basis.

4.2.2 Muslims' Awareness of Christians

The same question was asked to Muslims about Christians, in order to learn of their knowledge about Christians and how they relate to them. This category had five groups as well. The first 45% of Muslim respondents related that they knew of the Christian presence a long time ago[108] and this had enhanced early interaction with them as friends and neighbours on a daily basis. The following 23% of the Muslim respondents testified that they came to know Christians quite early in life when they were still young.

---

[107] Chawa CCAP views on Christian – Muslim relations, 08/2003.
[108] Thete Mosque views on Muslim – Christian relations, 10/2001.

While 15% of the respondents gained their knowledge of Christians through attending school together,[109] 10% of the respondents testified that they became acquainted with Christians because of doing business as partners or finding new settlements in the area of study. The last group of respondents (7%) said that they were not quite sure on how they came to know of the existence of Christians in the area. One thing they remembered was that they used to chase away Christian boys from their villages on religious grounds,[110] thus losing an opportunity for knowing people of a different faith.

4.2.3 General Perception

These findings may confirm to us that Muslims and Christians of the area under study are aware of each other's presence as neighbours, brothers and sisters, friends, relatives. They may not fully know of each other's religion but they accept the existence of each other and so are able to relate in harmony. As a result of this awareness, they are able to know what each of them is forbidden to eat. Christians are aware that Muslims do not eat pork[111] or any meat slaughtered without following the Islamic dietary tradition.

The same is true of Muslims who know that Christians eat pork, mice and any meat not slaughtered by following the Islamic dietary tradition. Although the Quran teaches that any meat slaughtered by "People of the Book" is acceptable (*halaal*) food,[112] Christians still invite Muslims to slaughter their cattle, goats or chicken for meat probably because of ignorance of that teaching or even for maintaining the already existing peaceful co-existence as people who invite each other to most of the functions taking place amongst them, for example funerals.[113]

---

[109] Chawa CCAP views on Christian – Muslim relations, 08/2003.
[110] Chitundu Mosque on Muslim-Christian relations, 08/2003.
[111] Chitundu CCAP views on Christian – Muslim relations, 08/2003.
[112] M.J. Kajawa, Personal Interview on Christian – Muslim relations, 08/2003.
[113] Ibid. Mualimu'- An Arabic word for a teacher.

They invite sheikhs or *'mualimu'* to slaughter their goats, chickens, or cattle probably for the concern they have for their Muslim neighbours, brothers and sisters or friends. This is especially true at the times of wedding parties, funerals, marriage engagements etc., where members of both religions are together and invite each other. Anyway, apart from the concern for Muslims, some people may feel that taking *'halaal'* meat makes them enjoy some spiritual blessing especially those surrounded by Muslim neighbours, probably those with Muslim relatives. This is where members of the same family cherishing two different religions meet.

4.2.4 Arguments based on logical deduction

Though the Muslims and Christians of this area are aware of the presence of each other as highlighted above, the following factors must have contributed to this welfare.[114] When Kamuzu Banda became the first president of Malawi encouraged Muslims to attend any school with the new government's educational policy, and also otherwise he attempted to give all religious groups prominence and a share in national achievement except the Jehovah's Witnesses who were really tortured and marginalized in Malawi despite emphasizing freedom of worship in the country. Muslims were encouraged to send their children to missions or government schools around Chitundu and Mthandiza congregations and the rest of the schools in the area.

His successor, Bakili Muluzi, went further by attending church services in the Christian churches. For example, Bakili Muluzi, while Head of State of the Republic of Malawi, attended church services at Nkhoma Mission congregation. On the first occasion he prayed with the congregation, then a rally followed, while the second

---

[114] David S. Bone, "*An Outline History of Islam in Malawi*", in David S. Bone (ed.), *Malawi's Muslims – Historical Perspectives*, Blantyre: CLAIM-Kachere, 2000, p. 21.

occasion was the induction ceremony of the then General Secretary of Nkhoma Synod CCAP, Winston R. Kawale, into his office.[115]

Sometimes Bakili Muluzi also attended funeral services in person or gave condolences to the bereaved, this he did regardless of religion. For example in October 2001 Muluzi attended the funeral service of late Hon. Chakakala Chaziya, a Christian and member of Lingadzi CCAP congregation at the time of his death. He was one of the prominent personalities in the government of Muluzi. The funeral sermon took place at his home congregation of Mang'a CCAP, the author attended and preached at the funeral service. This may have some influence upon the people of the area of study, seeing how freely the president, a Muslim, could interact with Christians at funerals within Nkhoma Synod CCAP. This was probably an incentive to consolidate the lifestyle of living in peace with people of other faiths or perhaps he was doing this because of his position in society as the leader of the country.

4.2.5 Mutual knowledge through festivals.

The introduction of the one Islamic festival (*Id-al Fitr*) as a public holiday in Malawi has also put Islam on the platform and people are able to say they have neighbours, the Muslims. For example during such festivals Muslims invite non-Muslims to such functions. At Linthipe, Thete, and Chitundu mosques some Christians attend the ceremonies.[116] In addition, Muslim men and women are openly dressing in the Islamic way these days. Muslims are also aware of the presence of Christians, this is seen in the observation of Christian festivals which are observed by Muslims. For example the Christmas festival which is observed in commemoration of the birth of Jesus whom Christians call Christ the Saviour of the world whom Muslims see as one of the prophets. In addition, Easter, which is in memory of the sufferings, death and resurrection of Jesus Christ

---

[115] The General Secretary's office, The Visitor's Book, 04.12.1994 and April 2001 respectively.
[116] Mayani Mosque views on Muslim-Christian relations, 08/2003.

are remembered, is well known to Muslims,[117] while on the other hand Muslims invite Christians to attend occasions like Islamic weddings. Because of this awareness probably that is why some Asians assist Christians to publish their Gospel music on CD's or cassettes or may be to make money.[118]

4.3 Relationships

The next question was on relationships regarding community development projects or politics of relation between the Christians and the Muslims of the area under study. This may be observed by looking at the co-operation or non-cooperation on development issues such as projects or politics that involve the people as one community. With the establishment of multiparty democracy in Malawi despite joining different parties this has not jeopardized the relationships of the people of the area under study. They can associate with different parties, still unity prevails at grassroots level, because the people, in spite of diversity in faith, are able to co-operate in other avenues on communal issues. Such issues would include day to day activities of attending each others' funerals, marriage-engagements or marriage ceremonies, helping each other in times of hunger' to mention a few.

In the preceding section, knowledge of each other has been emphasized. In this section we look at how they live together though of different faith and how they relate in instances of community projects, in times of crisis, in the market place, at marriage ceremonies and on issues of politics as examples.

4.3.1 Christian views

The views of Christians on interaction between them and Muslims stated that they were positive and that it was obvious to everyone

---

[117] Most Muslim respondents acknowledged their observation of such Christian festivals in the area of study.
[118] [17] G. Issa Premere Publications (Limbe), Naotcha CCAP Youth Fellowship Choir (Blantyre Synod CCAP) called "AYehova Tabwerani.".

in the area. Though the details of the teachings of Islam remain obscure to many Christians, the same is true of Muslims about Christianity. This has allowed the two religions to promote peaceful co-existence. This has so far been possible through dialogue between them. They are able to sit down and settle their differences.[119] They agree to disagree on matters of faith. There is respect for each other's religion.

About 60% of Christians interviewed testified that there are good relationships between them and the Muslims. In cases of any conflict, dialogue is the response to such situations in order to settle their differences so that peaceful co-existence is maintained at all cost.[120]

This is true of all the CCAP congregations in this area. Almost every church minister attested to the good relationship between Muslims and Christians in their respective congregations. Although such is the case, 20% of Christian respondents said that the relationship is fair with some exceptions. For example, one church minister complained of a predominant Muslim village where the graveyard committee is composed of Muslims only. And whenever a Muslim funeral occurs, the services held are orderly and take place in good time so that the mourners coming from afar can return to their respective homes in time. But when a Christian funeral takes place, the services are slow and this raises a lot of questions from the Christian mourners about such delays. At the time of interview the respondent stated that he was making arrangements for consultations with the responsible persons to put the matter right by either incorporating Christians in the graveyard committee or adhere to the complaint of treating the funeral services equally.[121]

---

[119] This is supported by Saidi Makande, Linthipe Mosque views on Muslim – Christian relations, 08/2003.
[120] Chitundu CCAP views on Christian – Muslim relations, 08/2003; Thete Mosque views on Muslim – Christian relations, 10/2001.
[121] Mnthandiza CCAP views on Christian – Muslim relations, 10/2001; 08/2003.

Another church minister complained that his sermon preached at a funeral was misinterpreted and then misunderstood. He preached from Exodus 13:19 and Genesis 50:25-26, passages with the story where the Israelites were advised to carry the bones of Joseph to Canaan in a coffin for reburial in Canaan. Some Muslims understood it as directed against them because they do not use coffins.[122]

In certain circumstances Christians were told to desist from marrying Muslim women.[123] This has changed for one is able to marry anyone he/she loves, like a Christian in one of the CCAP congregations married a Muslim lady who has been converted to Christianity. The husband has joined the holy ministry as a pastor and so she is a minister's wife.

Another 10% emphasized that the situation is not as bad as one may imagine, while 4% opted to say the opposite and the last group of 6% claimed that they were not sure.

In all the above issues, dialogue had an influence to modify circumstances. Where the two parties cannot face each other, a third party, usually traditional leaders,[124] are invited to settle matters in a manner befitting friends and neighbours in the same area. For example, at Thete market on the issue of selling pork, both the religious leaders and traditional leaders had to sit down to devise means to settle the dispute by providing a particular place in the market where pork would be sold without interference.

4.3.2 Muslim views

The same questions were asked to Muslims in order to know their views. This gave them the chance to express their views on how they look at their relationship with Christians and how they act on issues of community development and politics.

---

[122] Chawa CCAP views on Christian – Muslim relations, 10/2001.
[123] Mayani Mosque views on Muslim – Christian relations, 08/2003.
[124] Monekera CCAP views on Christian – Muslim relations, 08/2003.

Among those interviewed, five groups became apparent: 64% confirmed that there have always been good relationships and 15% claimed a fair relationship between Muslims and Christians in the area. The Muslims understand the differences that exist between them and Christians. Although there is religious diversity, they opt to co-exist in peace.

Further, 10% maintained that the situation is not all that bad while 7% said the opposite and the last group of 4% was not sure. Occasional situations of conflict are experienced. One lady respondent testified that in her life she has witnessed no conflict in the area under study except in Mangochi district where the issue was about Muslim women's dress; but the matter was settled through dialogue. She emphasized that she had never witnessed any conflicts in the area.[125] One sheikh complained that in 1953 some missionaries came to preach against Islam in their area around Linthipe.[126] On another occasion a Christian slaughtered a pig and sold its meat in an acceptable market place that really displeased Muslims. The issues were resolved through dialogue by traditional mediators.[127] It is obvious that Christians and Muslims live together in harmony; each group carrying out its own religious activities without provoking violence in the name of religion as is the case in other countries, for example northern Nigeria and Sudan, just to mention a few.

4.3.3 Manifestation of good relationships.

The good relationship can be seen in social activities taking place in the area, where Muslims and Christians perform tasks together without discrimination at all, while on the other hand they do not enjoy good relationship on doctrinal issues which are tackled from a different perspective but within the same context. They tolerate

---

[125] Mayani Mosque views on Muslim – Christian relations, 08/2003.
[126] Linthipe Mosque views on Muslim – Christian relations, 08/2003.
[127] Mayani Mosque views on Muslim – Christian relations, 08/2003.

each other in communal projects on one hand and doctrinal issues on the other within the area or village set up.

4.3.3.1 Social activities.

These are practical issues that members of either religion take part in on a daily basis, living as communities of Muslims and Christians. It is in these activities that the people express their relationship as people of one area living in harmony, regardless of their differences in faith. For example, in Chawa CCAP congregation at Lobi market both Muslims and Christians were able to buy from each other those goods acceptable by their respective religious beliefs. While at Mthandiza CCAP congregation Muslims and Christians help each other to bring the sick to the hospital when such an emergency occurs.

4.3.3.2 Community development.

Malawi as a developing nation has projects taking place in various parts in the country. This is true for the area under study. In Mphunzi CCAP congregation, both Muslims and Christians moulded bricks for a community day secondary school and a health clinic.[128] In another congregation, Mthandiza CCAP, Muslims supported Christians in the burning of bricks for a CCAP church building.[129]

In some places, road and borehole maintenance is done by both Christians and Muslims working together regardless of religion.[130] In such cases village headmen or traditional leaders take a special lead in committees of the community projects where Muslims and Christians work together in unison and harmony.

One respondent, a church minister who was once a leader of Nkhoma Synod, stated that in community projects where members of the two religions work together, very good relationships

---

[128] Mphunzi CCAP views on Christian – Muslim relations, 10/2001.
[129] Mnthandiza CCAP views on Christian – Muslim relations, 10/2001.
[130] Linthipe Mosque, views on Muslim – Christian relations, 08/2003.

prevail.¹³¹ In these projects like community day secondary schools, road maintenance, clearing roads, etc, total co-operation between members of these religions is observed. But two respondents pointed out that Muslims work better on *madrassa* projects or those that are for Muslims only than community projects involving Christians and Muslims.¹³²

This compels one to believe that cooperation among Muslims and Christians is propelled by nationalist sentiment, but religious sentiment is higher when it comes to faith based projects.

4.3.3.3 Entrepreneurship.

The selling and buying of commodities from each other affects both Christian and Muslim communities. Almost 90% of all the respondents from either group confirmed that they do business in the same markets and trading centers respectively. To avoid conflicts, the selling of pork is given a special place in the vicinity of the same market where Muslims may not go.

About 100% of Muslim respondents had reservations about pork. According to Islamic teaching, Muslims are not allowed to eat pork because it is *haram (unacceptable meat for Muslims)*. Therefore, they agreed that pork should be sold at a specific place outside the market whereas goats, chicken, sheep, cattle are slaughtered in the Islamic tradition by a Muslim to allow both Muslims and Christians to eat such meat.¹³³

4.3.3.4 Politics.

Almost 70% of the respondents of either religion confirmed that all participate in politics freely, regardless of religion.¹³⁴ Members of

---

[131] Nkhoma Synod Offices, Likuni, views on Christian – Muslim relations, 08/2003 while he was in the Head Office as General Secretary of Nkhoma Synod at Nkhoma Mission station.
[132] A.A. Sasu, on Christian – Muslim relations, while serving as the General Secretary of Nkhoma Synod CCAP.
[133] Mayani Mosque views on Muslim – Christian relations, 10/2001.
[134] Mphunzi CCAP views on Christian – Muslim relations, 10/2001.

either religion are free to join any political party, be it UDF, MCP, AFORD etc. Some 20% Muslim respondents said that United Democratic Front is a clan party for them because the leader is a Muslim while Christians are for the Malawi Congress Party or Alliance for Democracy.[135]

About 10% respondent went further to say that UDF is for the Yao tribe, MCP for the Chewa and AFORD for people in the North (Tumbuka, Tonga, Ngoni etc).[136]

4.3.3.5 Marriage celebrations.

The respondents testified that marriage ceremonies or engagements are a common feature among the people of the different religions in this area, especially among Muslims and Christians. Therefore, 80% of the respondents reported that they attend such functions regardless of religion while 15% of either religion stated that they attend upon invitation, and that it is only then that they can contribute towards the expenses of the function in form of money or other gifts.[137] The last 5% of the respondents were neutral. The only reservations are on issues of rituals. This is left to members of the religion responsible for religious services. Friends and neighbours in the vicinity remain passive although they are not denied attendance of the functions in either case.

4.3.3.6 Times of crisis.

In times of crisis such as funerals, HIV and AIDS pandemic, TB, malaria, etc, the first 90% of Christian and Muslim respondents agreed that all people in the vicinity attend funeral ceremonies regardless of religion.[138] To show their hospitality as neighbours and friends they contribute food, money, firewood to help one another. The only thing that demarcates their relationship is religion. They

---

[135] Yao, belongs to UDF because the leader is a Muslim, 10/2001.
[136] UDF - Yao, MCP - Chewa and Aford for the north for Tumbuka and Ngoni, 10/2001.
[137] Mayani Mosque views on Muslim – Christian relations, 08/2003.
[138] Monekera CCAP views on Christian – Muslim relations, 08/2003.

allow the concerned party to carry out the ritual service while others remain as observers. But no member of either religion is denied attendance at the funeral service at all.

On the question of diseases, especially the HIV and AIDS pandemic that has not spared the people of the area, all respondents agreed that they are involved in preaching the same message that "prevention is better than cure" as there is no medicine available yet for the pandemic.[139] In addition, those infected are cared for either by visiting or caring for them as the need arises. The HIV and Aids policy of the government and that of the CCAP General Assembly consolidate the work of looking after the sick.[140] For other diseases like TB, malaria, cholera, Christians and Muslims preach the same message of prevention and encourage their members to maintain hygienic standards wherever possible and to attend health clinics as early as possible.

These examples of activities suffice to express the attitude of Christians and Muslims, that despite diversity in religious affairs, they nevertheless work together amicably for peaceful co-existence.

4.3.3.7 Doctrinal issues.

It is not only in social matters that Muslims and Christians co-operate, but in doctrinal issues as well. This is probably so because of the freedom of worship that the late President Hastings Kamuzu Banda emphasized in his speeches. Freedom of worship was always there well before the coming of the Ngwazi, but he articulated it for the sake of unity. This initially laid foundations for tolerance between religions. The examples below suffice to explain the situation in the vicinity.

---

[139] Monekera CCAP views on Christian – Muslim relations, 10/2001; 08/2003.
[140] CCAP General Assembly, HIV and AIDS Policy, 'Love, Care and Compassion, Head Office, Lilongwe, 2004.

4.3.3.8 Revival meetings or Dawah.

These are meetings organized by either of the religions in the area. They are publicized by inviting church leaders, traditional leaders and people with positions in the government sector or in business. The meetings are open to all and are held in the open air. They usually have a theme on a specific issue. This is where a religion propagates itself according to its beliefs and understanding. The members of the religion are strengthened in their faith and non-members are challenged to make a decision to accept the teachings of the religion. This is probably seen as an opportunity for fellowship and propagation of the religion and not a source of conflict

4.3.3.9 Funeral services.

Another area that affects doctrinal matters are funeral services where all people are summoned to attend the service regardless of religious affiliation. They come with gifts like maize flour, chicken, firewood, money and other services to help at the funeral. The ritual aspect is left in the hands of the religion concerned. The other attendants remain passive until the whole service and burial is over.

4.3.3.10 Dress.

The members of either religion are free to dress as their religion demands. Muslim men and women are free to dress according to the demands of their religion. Their expression of religious status is not denied or frowned upon, which may not be possible in other countries.

4.3.3.11 Visitation.

Visitation also plays a role in propagating either of the religions especially in times of bereavement and sickness. Visits to the poor or the elderly and sometimes in normal friendship are occasions where in a casual way one may say something in relation to his/her religion. This is practiced by both sides.

4.3.3.12 Religious festivals.

Both religions have remarkable festivals. In Christianity we have Christmas in memory of the birth of Jesus Christ and Easter when the suffering, death and resurrection of Jesus Christ are commemorated, while Muslims have such religious festivals as *Id al-Fitr, Id al-adhah,*. On such occasions religious beliefs are propagated because of the activities that go with every celebration.

4.3.3.13 Synthesis.

What transpires from the above discussion may probably show that freedom of worship is accepted in the area by both religions. This is why relationship testified in matters of sickness or bereavement. In such circumstances both Muslims and Christians may bring to each other gifts like firewood, maize flour and even money when the other things are not available. The expression of religious status is not denied in the area for Muslim women are free to dress as Muslims, festivals observed as per the religious affiliation to which one belongs either at Christmas or Id - al – Fitr time. Because of such an atmosphere, dialogue of the faith groups is tolerated among the people.

4.4 Nkhoma Synod's admission policy

CCAP Nkhoma Synod model of approach would probably reflect PROCMURA's way of doing things as M.J. Kajawa pastored in all congregations in the area under study except Nkhoma and Mphunzi congregations with his experience of PROCMURA. Therefore, his influence may have impact of doing things.

This has probably enabled the Synod promoting good relationships in sharing her resources For example, all her schools like William Murray, Mlanda Girls, Mvera Girls, Msonkhamanja, Nkhoma Community Secondary Schools are open to all students without segregation. Another resource open to all is the Nkhoma Hospital and her outer clinics which are attended by all people, regardless of religion. And a good number of Muslims come to

Nkhoma hospital from all around the area under study and beyond for treatment.

The other resource the Synod shares is employment in her departments where people are employed according to merit and not religious affiliation. At one time the foreman of the building department was a Muslim. Some of these sometimes gradually accept Jesus as Lord and Saviour.

With the Malawi government policy on the HIV and AIDS pandemic through the National Aids Commission, all people are encouraged to join hands to fight the disease. This encourages members of both religions to work together for the good of the nation and so enables them to relate to each other. An example are home based care centers owned by Nkhoma congregation for people living with HIV and AIDS and the issue of orphans who are cared for under the auspices of the HIV and AIDS department and the orphan care department. These do not look into the religion one belongs to or his /her religious affiliation. In addition the members of parliament of this area under study take part in encouraging and supporting such groups in their respective constituencies.

4.5 Witnessing for the religion

Adherents of both Islam and Christianity are mandated to witness for their respective religions to non-members. This helps the religion to grow and win new members to their group. Therefore, questions were asked to find out how their religions reach out to people, which methods are used and what probably might be the ideal one.

4.5.1 Christian views.

The Christian respondents pointed out a few methods that help the spread of Christianity in the area as it competes with the Islamic religion. The following examples were cited by the Christian respondents:

4.5.1.1 Revival meetings.

Once in a while, every Nkhoma Synod congregation conducts revival meetings to call people to Christ or to revive the faith of members. Such meetings usually take place in summer. In most cases three to five meetings may take place per year depending on the needs of a particular congregation. As a means of evangelism, non-Christians, Muslims inclusive and traditional leaders and members of other faiths are also invited to such occasions. This does not exclude the already committed members.[141] Therefore, attendance occurs because of invitation or attraction through choirs or the theme of the revival meeting. In one congregation the sound system is used to call people to such meetings; when they hear choirs singing are attracted to hear more. It becomes a chance for sharing the Good News to all, regardless of religion.

4.5.1.2 Preaching through individual visitations.

Some respondents pointed out that individual visitations play a greater role in portraying to their counterparts the belief to which one belongs to. This may take different forms like visiting the sick, the bereaved, the aged, the orphans and others. Such visits may include everyone in the area regardless of religion. These visits go with the word of God and prayer depending on circumstances. The advantage of this method is that it reveals true concern when one is visited. Therefore, individual visitations help in conversation where questions and answers are received and responded to in love.[142]

4.5.1.3 Preaching at funeral services.

Almost 90% of the Christian respondents confirmed that preaching at a Christian funeral service is regarded as a method of witnessing to Muslims. When asked why it can be classified as one of the ideal methods, they stressed that it gives an opportunity for evangelism

---

[141] Mphunzi CCAP views on Christian – Muslim relations, 10/2001.
[142] Mphunzi CCAP views on Christian – Muslim relations, 10/2001.

because all people around the area or village come to attend the funeral service besides all the relatives who may be believers or not. All people come regardless of religion. The non-believers would not dare to enter a church or a Christian fellowship, but attending a funeral service is imperative.[143]

This is probably because Africans like to live together as a community and always like to help one another in times of joy or trouble or perhaps for fear of being outcasts in times of need. If one is noticed that he does not attend other people's funerals he is punished by the community. People may boycott his funeral or that of his relatives.

When a Christian funeral occurs, the Good News is preached to all though members of other faiths remain passive in matters of rituals.[144] The same is true when a Muslim funeral occurs. The message from the Quran is preached to all attending the service. However, the underlying factor is that those who accept Jesus as Lord and Saviour or the message from the Quran through these services are free to join the church or mosque. The 90% Christian respondents supported the method because it does not bar any particular individual to listen to the messages preached to the particular group. Though, there was nothing specific about the Zyala expreicitly mentioned but is celebrated.

4.5.2 Muslim views

Muslims agree to the first and the last method applied by Christians: preaching at a Muslim funeral service and revival meetings *(Dawah)*. The respondents emphasized funeral services in that people come to attend a funeral regardless of religion or because perhaps Africans are understood as a community people who tend to be together in times of joy or sadness regardless of

---

[143] e.g. Daison Phiri of Mphunzi CCAP.
[144] Linthipe Mosque views on Muslim – Christian relations, 08/2003.
   Zyala=It should be noted that the visit to the tombs of holy men or saints in Islam has a Christian parallel in the visit to Jerusalem.

religion or ethnic grouping.[145] One respondent added marriage as another factor for conversion. When a male Muslim marries a non - Muslim lady, the children born to this family become Muslims automatically according to the rules of the Islamic faith; probably this could reflect the African way of community as Africans are a community people.[146]

Some respondents put forward *Zyala* as another method for spreading Islam in the area where non - Muslims are invited to attend such functions.[147] In some instances they have experienced conversion from Christianity to Islam. In one congregation there were five lady converts from Christianity to Islam probably through *Zyala*. Some respondents expressed the view that they have never experienced or seen any conversion arising from the *Zyala*. One respondent stated that there is no need for evangelism or witnessing as the ideal method would be silence because every religion points to the One God, and to eternal life with God.[148]

4.6. Ideal method

Most Muslim and Christian respondents expressed the opinion that the ideal method to witness for one's religion is through dialogue,[149] because dialogue shows love and concern for the other party and that one is able to listen to the opposing views without interruption. Dialogue creates an atmosphere of care both physically and spiritually. The approach of dialogue encourages learning from one another, for there is openness, mutual respect and confidence in each other with freedom of expression of faith enhanced by peaceful co-existence as people of one area.

---

[145] Chitundu CCAP views on Christian – Muslim relations, 08/2003.
[146] John S.m\Mbiti, *Introduction to African Religion*, Nairobi: Heinemann, 1978.
[147] Mayani Mosque views on Muslim – Christian relations, 08/2003.
[148] Ibid.
[149] Mayani Mosque views on Muslim – Christian relations, 08/2003.

4.6.1 Synthesis

It may appear that proselytism and implicit dialogue in action co-exist in the area under study. This may be true or may not because dialogue in this context could be understood at two levels. The first is that people are free to express their faith without fearing anything; the challenge is that there is freedom of worship and expression that people may hear or see or accept whatever touches their hearts.

The second is when an individual is touched by the message and therefore makes a choice of which religion to follow, the individual is free to do so. Though elsewhere in Islam one may be denied support or get killed by parents or relatives or fellow adherents once converted to another religion, this is unheard of in the area under study.

The third level is not utilized yet to a large extent where both Muslims and Christians would be able to sit down together to discuss doctrinal issues for clarity amicably yet living in diversity but co-existing in peace.

The above issue is not fully utilized as intended except for discussing community development projects or HIV/AIDS pandemic issues or in times of funerals, to mention a few. The former idea is an opportunity for consolidating the relationship even when conversion may not be in sight.

4.7 Conflict resolution

The questions were asked to find out what happens when conflict occurs and, if such is the case, how resolutions are reached. It was a challenging question, because of some countries in Africa we always hear over the radio or read in newspapers of the fights between the two religions, therefore, the issue of peace between Christians and Muslims is questionable, like in Sudan or northern Nigeria.[150] In many cases members of these religions fight and even

---

[150] Through the Media, especially Malawi Broadcasting Cooperation (MBC).

kill each other, for the sake of religion. Then, how are Muslims and Christians of this area able to relate peacefully while practicing their religions freely?

This question arises because conflicts elsewhere in Africa are reported in the media and even in Malawi conflicts happened, like the burning of mosques in the Northern Region by Christians, the attack on a Roman Catholic priest and the burning down of his car, or the attacks on Christian churches in Mangochi district.[151] That these attacks happened was most likely due to political reasons. Nothing like that happened in the area of study, but can it be spared forever?

4.7.1 Christian conflict experience

Three pastors expressed that they had never experienced conflict with Muslims during the time they had been in their respective congregations[152] while one pastor experienced some misunderstanding that occurred after his sermon at a funeral. The issue centered on the carrying of the bones of Joseph in a coffin from Egypt to Canaan. It was misinterpreted as if it was preached against Muslims because Muslims do not use coffins.[153]

Another pastor complained over one predominantly Muslim village where Christians are in the minority that has a graveyard committee whose members are Muslims only. Whenever there is a Muslim funeral, the services are fast and smooth and whenever there is a Christian funeral the services are slow, but when there is a Muslim funeral people get organized and the grave is dug in time and the burial is in time and mourners are released in time so that those who come from afar are able to return to their respective

---

[151] *Malawi News* 2004; Ibrahim Milazi, "The Burning of Mosques in the North: Is it the Beginning or Climax of Political Fanaticism or of Christian Fundamentalism in Malawi?", *Religion in Malawi* no 9 (1999), p. 42.

[152] Malawi News/Daily Times, 1994 and 2004. The Sunday Times, 24th February, 2008, p. 7.

[153] Mphunzi CCAP views on Christian – Muslim relations, 08/2003.

homes in time.[154] To the contrary, a Christian funeral might take longer time for the rest of the work to complete and so burial services are delayed and mourners depart late from the grave yard and those coming from afar end up reaching their respective homes very late.

Therefore, the Christians complain about the practice. Other respondents had experienced conflicts over burial ceremonies where Christian boys were chased away from nearby Muslim villages. A pastor from another congregation heard a Muslim youth prevented from entering a Christian village.[155] In another instance Christians were not allowed to marry Muslim women because their Muslim counterparts could not accept Christians to marry Muslim ladies. Thirdly, at a political rally a pastor saw a Muslim politician insulting a Christian opposition leader.[156] At a lower level some respondents had conflicts on doctrinal issues like at Mayani market in Chitundu congregation where a quarrel erupted out on the issue of selling pork at the wrong place.[157] In addition, there were two lady respondents who had conflicts with two female Christian youths who wanted to get married to Muslims boys.[158] The parents were not willing to allow them to get married on religious grounds. One respondent expressed his sadness over the attitude of superiority that some Muslims have towards members of other religions, whom they usually call "Kaffirs."[159] One respondent mentioned selling pork in an unspecified location in a market, which caused a verbal fight.[160]

---

[154] Chawa CCAP views on Christian – Muslim relations, 10/2001.
[155] Mnthandiza CCAP views on Christian – Muslim relations, 10/2001.
[156] Mayani Mosque views on Muslim – Christian relations, 08/2003.
[157] Chitundu CCAP views on Christian – Muslim relations, 08/2003.
[158] , Chitundu CCAP views on Christian – Muslim relations, 08/2003.
[159] Mfumu (Village Headman) Chayera, Chitundu CCAP views on Christian – Muslim relations, 08/2003.
[160] Mayani Mosque views on Muslim – Christian relations, 08/2003.

On political issues, some thought that all Yao belonged to the United Democratic Front in this area while Chewa and Ngoni were members of the Malawi Congress Party.

The last group, the majority of respondents, a combination from different congregations, expressed absence of conflicts in their respective congregations and villages. That meant there had always been Muslims and Christians in the area under study living together without tension.

4.7.2 Muslim views on conflict experience.

Muslims had their own stories to tell in response to what Christians said about conflict experience. One sheikh responded that once he saw white missionaries in 1953 from Nkhoma coming to his area in full force to preach against Islam.[161] This caused suspicion in the eyes of Muslims.

Another sheikh experienced confrontations with Christians on why the prophet Muhammad has a large following yet he died, and his grave can be traced today, unlike Jesus who died, was buried and rose again from the dead and ascended into heaven?[162]

Another sheikh stated that he used to chase away Christian boys from his village because of religion.[163] One Muslim had experienced a conflict with a certain Phiri who slaughtered a pig in 1985 and sold it at an unacceptable place in their community market.

Another group of Muslim respondents testified that they know no conflict with Christians, while yet another group of respondents stressed that they do not expect any conflict to take place at all with Christians in their area. The last group heard nothing of conflict and does not think of any to take place.[164] This reveals that about 44% of Muslims who experience conflict with Christians is minimal, compared to those who claim that there are continued good relationships with Christians despite diversity in faith.

---

[161] Linthipe Mosque views on Muslim – Christian relations, 08/2003.
[162] Mnthandiza CCAP, views on Christian – Muslims Relations, 08/2003.
[163] Mayani Mosque views on Muslim – Christian relations, 08/2003.
[164] Lobi Mosque views on Muslim – Christian relations, 08/2003.

4.7.3 Conflict resolution.

By looking at the different views from Muslim and Christian perspectives, there are some who have experienced some conflicts. For example, one respondent commented that in the time of the Malawi Congress Party government there was a good relationship but things changed with the coming of the United Democratic Front government because of political membership has been politicized and these affect the welfare of the community in the area.

The third group claims no expectation of conflict even for the future between them. But the question still stands: how do they resolve conflicts that arise between them? One Muslim respondent asserted that the thought of conflict in this area is remote and does not expect any conflict to take place in the near future in their area.[165]

When you look at the different views of the respondents, you will see that at every conflict that occurred they applied the method of dialogue. Two opposing parties sat face to face directly to resolve their differences. If necessary, traditional leaders were invited to settle the matter through dialogue. Thus, in all cases dialogue has played the greatest role. Dialogue allows them to face each other to promote peace so that co-existence between Muslims and Christians continues to be peaceful. Good example is when a Christian sold pork at an inappropriate place in the area of Chitundu congregation at their local market, the members of the two religions and some traditional leaders met and settled the issue amicably.

4.7.3.1 General perception

According to the findings, one may conclude that conflicts may occur probably because of personality clashes. This is so because the majority of Christians and Muslims live side by side. But generally few conflicts are expected. Although the people are living in religious diversity there is respect for one another and peaceful

---

[165] Chawa CCAP views on Christian – Muslim relations, 08/2003.

co-existence between them without hindering each other in the spread of their religions.

4.8 Basis for unity

> "Unity among Malawians in this is area is based on tradition or clan other than religion"

This section will highlight the basis for unity for Muslims and Christians of this area against the statement that says, "Unity among Malawians is based on tradition or clan rather than on religion."

The discussion in this chapter has so far shown that Muslims and Christians co-exist in peace. The question can arise, how is this unity possible? Is it as a result of religion or tradition? The statement has two facets: unity based on tradition or clan and unity based on religion. Any conflict attitude is probably brought by foreign people to the area.

4.8.1 Christian views on unity.

Some 70% of Christian respondents said that unity is based on religion.[166] They support religion because of the change of cultural climatic conditions that are apparent every day towards individualistic life style. One respondent of the same view proved his point by saying that unity is changing its course and is going towards mutual relations based on common interests of ideas and beliefs, thus "religion."[167] While 20% of the respondents said that unity is based on tradition, they still perceived members to be free to maintain their religious identities of being a Muslim or a Christian. Therefore, to this group, tradition is the major source of unity because Muslims (Yao) have their own villages, the Chewa and the Ngoni too. In that context tradition is more binding because

---

[166] Chawa CCAP views on Christian – Muslim relations, 08/2003.
[167] Monekera CCAP views on Christian – Muslim relations, 08/2003.

it is in the blood.[168] Further 5% of the Christian respondents were not sure of what the unity is based on; their minds wavered between the two points. The fourth group of respondents of 3% was not sure.

4.8.2 Muslim views on unity.

Some 60% of Muslim respondents admitted that unity is based on religion in this area because each religious group goes together, like Muslims, Christians, and African Traditional Religionists. But this does not prevent them from relating to each other in instances of communal interest that affect all, e.g. funerals. In that aspect religion forms a solid unity in the area.

However, one respondent stated that unity in this area is based on tradition because tradition is the major source of unity, for villages are grouped according to families of the same blood, be they Yao, Chewa or Ngoni, though the picture has been diversified through inter-marriage. Members of these groups, though divided by tribe, are free to affiliate with any religious group, Christianity or Islam while maintaining traditional backgrounds. John Mbiti writes, "When an African is in crisis he goes home to consult his clan people of how to go about the problem, regardless of either high education or other religious affiliations."[169],

4.8.3. Common unity.

In this respect, tradition tends to bind people together more than the missionary religions, though every community has both Muslims and Christians. For example, both Christians and Muslims are able to attend each other's activities, the reason being that of tradition and this gives an opportunity to hear of the missionary religions. For the case of Malawi, sometimes both tribalistic and regionalistic attitudes play a part. Therefore, because of the

---

[168] A.A. Sasu, Nkhoma Synod Offices, while serving as the General Secretary of Nkhoma Synod CCAP -(Likuni) views on Christian – Muslim relations, 08/2003.

[169] John S. Mbiti, *Introduction to African Religion*, Nairobi: Heinemann, 1978, p. 192.

opportunity of living in diversity enjoyed by everyone in the area, it is probable indication that the PROCMURA model of approach has an influence upon the people in dialogue promotes living in diversity in mutual relationship with the fact that the proponent of PROCMURA approach, M.J.Kajawa, served in most of the congregations of Chitundu and her daughter congregation Makungubwi, Mthandiza, Monekera and her daughter congregation Madalitso and Chawa respectively.

4.8.4 Synthesis.

Though it appears there are opposing views on tradition and religion, the truth is that the two religions interact with each other freely. Tradition binds the people at the base while being a Muslim or Christian comes above. But African Traditional Religion is within the blood. In the Malawi context, especially in this area under study, tradition and religion go together but with different functions in the community..

FIG 4.1a
KNOWLEDGE OF MUSLIMS
Christians awareness of muslims

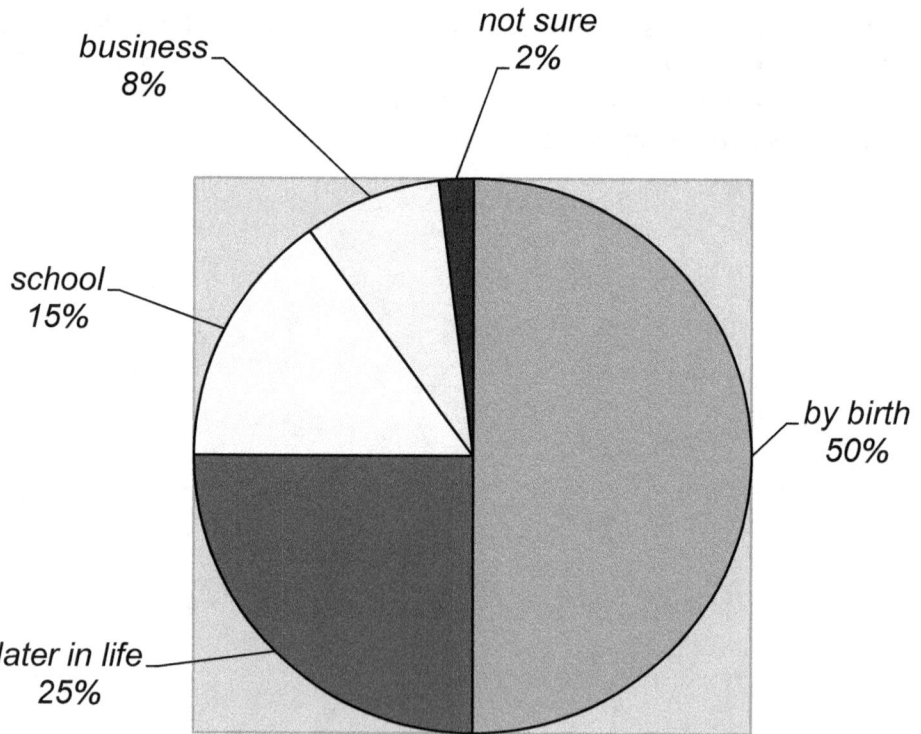

FIG 4.1b:
KNOWLEDGE OF CHRISTIANS
Muslims awareness of christians

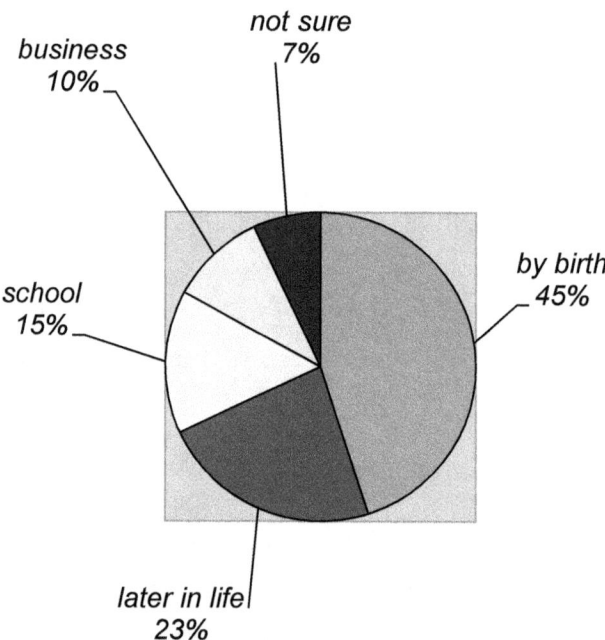

FIG 1a:
KNOWLEDGE OF MUSLIMS
Christians awareness of muslims

**FIG 1a:
KNOWLEDGE OF MUSLIMS
Christians awareness of muslims**

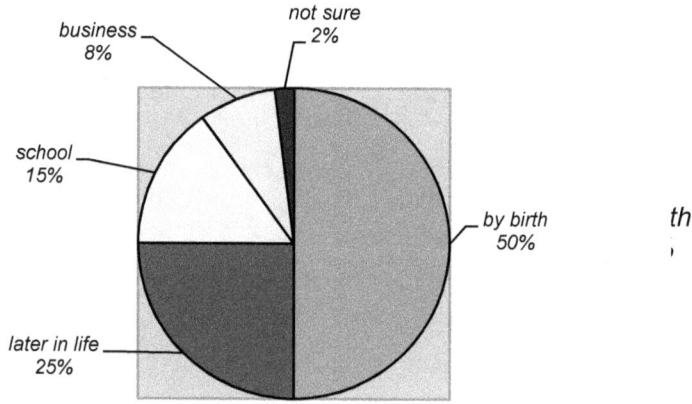

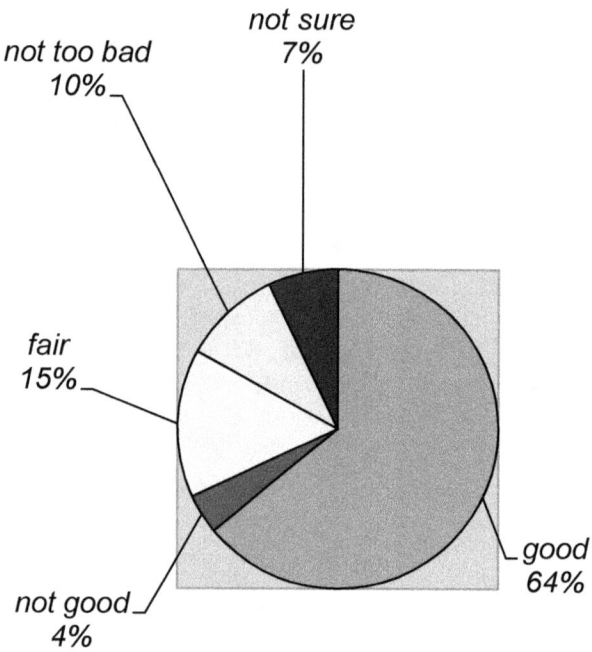

FIG 4. 3a:
WITNESSING FOR RELIGION
Christians views

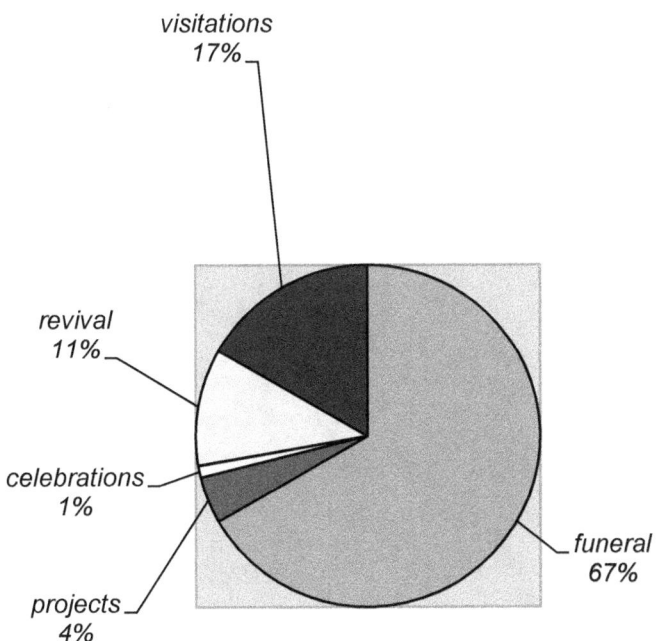

**FIG 4. 3b:
WITNESSING FOR RELIGION
Muslims views**

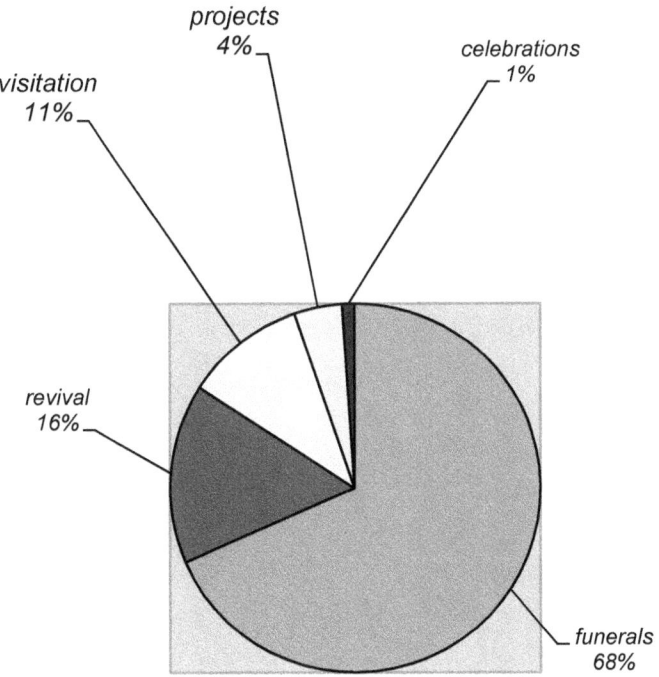

FIG 4. 4a:
CONFLICT EXPERIENCE
Christians views

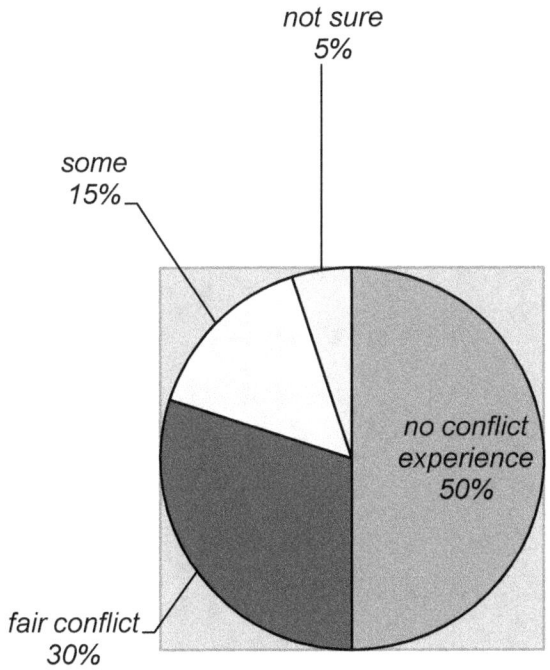

FIG 4.4b:
CONFLICT EXPERIENCE
Muslims views

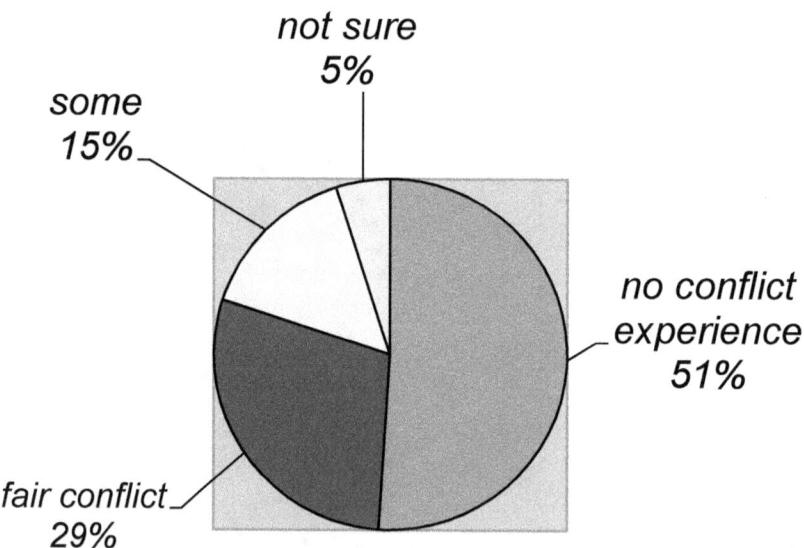

FIG 4. 5a:
THE BASIS FOR UNITY
Christians views

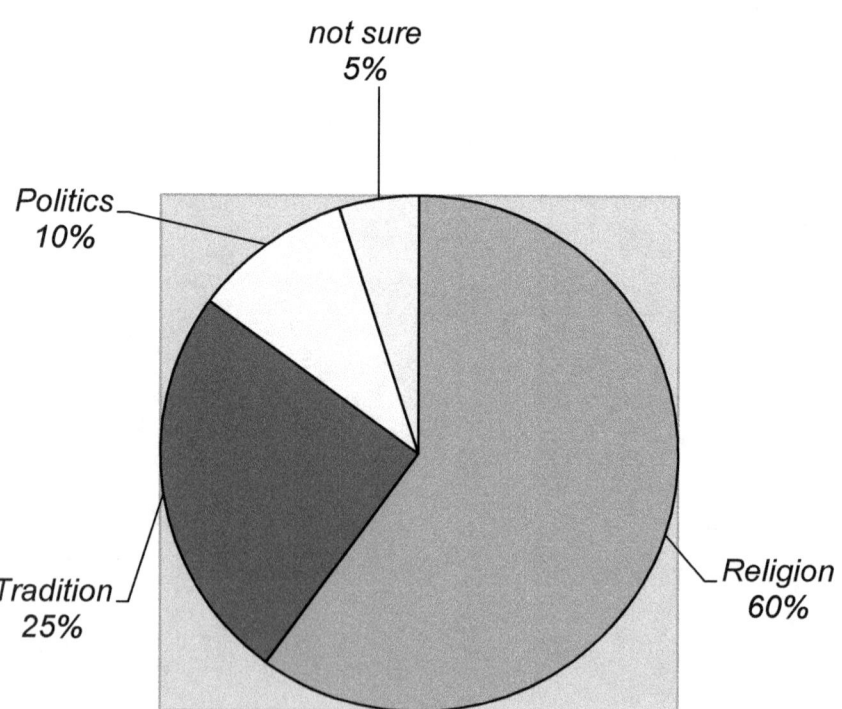

FIG 4. 5b:
THE BASIS FOR UNITY
Muslims views

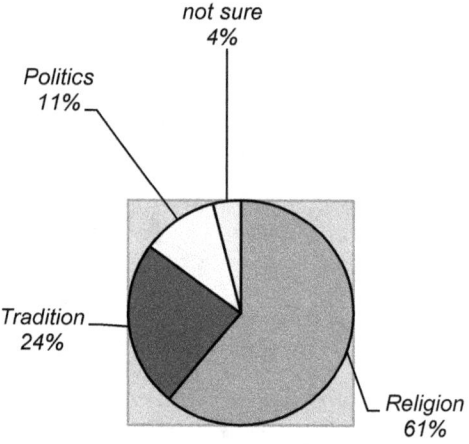

Chapter Four

Dialogue: a prerequisite for peaceful co-existence for Malawi Muslims and Christians

5.1 Introduction

Discussions in this chapter prompt us to consider dialogue as a crucial aspect to be encouraged, promoted and supported by Malawi Muslims and Christians if we want to worship and co-exist in diversity but peacefully. Though there has been fighting in countries like Sudan and Northern Nigeria, and elsewhere we discover that the general consensus shows and proves in this book, that it is possible for both religious faith groups to co-exist as demanded by the laws and constitution of the Republic of Malawi.[170]

Almost all Christians and Muslims interviewed agree that dialogue is the ideal answer if peace needs to be maintained and that freedom of worship can still exist in diversity. This view is held in spite of earlier cases of antagonism. For example, around Chitundu Christian boys were being chased from Muslim villages. On other hand, in 1953 missionaries from Nkhoma preached against Islam at Linthipe One in Dedza. Therefore, there was and still is need for a paradigm shift of attitudes for Malawi Muslims and Christians[171] from that of prejudice and antagonism to dialogue especially with the presence of a multi-party system of government prevailing today, which permits freedom of worship, expression and association.[172]

---

[170] Ministry of Justice, *The Constitution of the Republic of Malawi*, Malawi Government Press, Zomba, 2004, p. 21.
[171] Mfumu (Village Headman) Chayera, Chitundu CCAP views on Christian – Muslim relations, 08/2003; Umali Mkaliwa, Linthipe Mosque, Views on Muslim-Christian relations, 08/2003.
[172] Robert Phiri, Public Affairs Committee Report 2003, p. 5.

The Dutch Reformed Church missionaries emphasized conversion at first without consideration of dialogue at all. It was only from the 1950s to the present period that a moderate view was embraced by the Synod of Nkhoma. This positive attitude accepts dialogue as a new approach to inter-faith relations embodying the principle that is utilized by PROCMURA. This is apparent in this area probably due to the influence of A.G. van Wyk when he established Chitundu congregation upon his return from Egypt after his training in Islamic studies or perhaps it is due to M.J. Kajawa who pastored in almost all congregations with Muslim communities in the area researched.[173]

What remains for the Synod today is endorsement and encouragement of dialogue in its approach to other faith groups, Muslims inclusive. This principle is also encouraged by the World Council of Churches and the All Africa Conference of Churches. Both of these organizations have inter-faith desks. Therefore, if CCAP Nkhoma Synod wants to succeed in her mission to people of other faith communities she has to embark on civic education about dialogue which is important for its members so that the church continues to maintain such a stand of sharing the Good news and avoid a repeat of the crusades.[174]

The Church has to be pro-active in dialogue for the sake of the Gospel. It is essential to start from the known to the unknown so that fruitful dialogue takes place.[175] For example both religions, Christianity and Islam, claim Abraham as their ancestor. Further, the last judgment, the second coming of Jesus, prophets are taught in both religions, except for the diversity in interpretation, which can only be understood through dialogue.

Muslims and Christians live side by side in the same village, doing the same business together in the same market, attend each other's funerals, work together in all community projects,

---

[173] M.J. Kajawa, Personal Interview, 08/2003.
[174] M.J. Kajawa, personal Interview, 08/2003.
[175] M.J. Kajawa, Personal interview, 08/2003.

cooperate in times of crisis such as poverty and the HIV and AIDS pandemic, all of which affect lives of people regardless of religion. In such circumstances one asks, how should Muslims and Christians continue to relate to each other better as Malawians, yet in diversity of religious beliefs? The answer is dialogue.[176] But for dialogue to take place a few things must happen especially when people accept one another as equals in the sight of God. That process is called 'communication', the basis for maximum success in dialogue. This helps Muslims and Christians to understand each other better.

5.2 Inter-faith dialogue

The question of mission or inter-faith dialogue is dealt with through the process of communication that members of both religions benefit from. In summary, dialogue involves two parties or more as partners. Dialogue for our purpose is defined as happening between partners who accept that they are equal in diversity.

This signifies that each knows his/her limits and accepts the other as a partner. The two parties are due to share their agenda and so enter into dialogue. We cannot co-exist in our societies and decide to ignore each other; for better or for worse; we are bound to relate and we should relate positively and so we can understand each other better.[177] If that is the case then, the two principles for Christian – Muslim relations in Africa apply. The first principle is:

> "To promote among the churches in Africa faithful and responsible Christian witness in an inter-faith environment of Christians and Muslims that will promote and not unduly jeopardize the spirit of good neighbourliness."

While the second principle states,

---

[176] Kaliza, Personal Interview, 10/2001.
[177] Haggai Institute (Singapore), Lecture notes on Communications, 1995.

> "To promote Christian constructive engagement with Muslims, so that together, members of the two communities can work towards the promotion of peace and peaceful coexistence, and embark on joint actions on issues that militate against the development of society."[178]

5.2.1 Challenges of dialogue.

Dialogue is required in the world today for the sake of world peace. Therefore it needs to be looked at cautiously from all angles of life. Though such is the case there are challenges that try to hinder the process of inter-faith dialogue for communities to relate to each other in harmony. One of the challenges is the failing of the paradigm shift away from an attitude of antagonism when entering into inter-faith dialogue.

The moment that the heart of humility is missing, it automatically switches off the welcoming heart to receive the message. For example, Andrew Kaufa writes of a Roman Catholic catechist who once said,

> "We live peacefully with Muslims here; they borrow our stretcher (*Geneza*) for their funeral functions etc. But for me dialogue smells of heresy. We can mislead Christians."[179]

This implies that dialogue is dangerous and that people can easily be misled. This, probably, reveals the attitude of many a church leader. They prefer shunning away from dialogue. The second hurdle is perception. The moment perception is not conducive for understanding how things are, dialogue will not apply.

For example, if you look at the picture on page 95 you will discover that at the first glance you will not be able to distinguish

---

[178] PROCMURA, *Strategic Plan 2007/8 – 2011/12*, p. 4.
[179] Andrew U. Kaufa, *Muslim – Christian Dialogue: A Challenge to Christian Churches in Malawi*, University of Malawi, Department of Theology and Religious Studies, June 1993, p. 16.

whether there is one picture or more, but as you look closely, you will discover that there are two pictures, that of an old lady and that of a young lady within the same picture. If you do the same with the picture on page 96 your first glance will show a tumbler or a candle holder but looking closely you will see two people facing each other.

These two examples suffice to explain that you do not understand a person at the first meeting, but when dialogue develops, only then you come to understand one another better.[180] The third hurdle to dialogue is the attitude of superiority, where the recipient is taken as passive or empty or an object. No human being remains passive on issues of communication, for human beings are meant to respond to every message received either verbally or otherwise in whatever manner. In one way or other the recipient shall always respond negatively or positively to every message that comes to her or him.

5.3 Communication as a catalyst

Dialogue shall not take place unless a process of communication is available just as no car moves unless it has petrol. This communication can be defined as the mutual exchange of information and understanding by effective means. Such dialogue has to be accompanied by the process of communication if it is to take its course and make sense. In this regard communication has three elements in order to complete the process i.e. *the sender* or *source*, the *message* and *the recipient*; and they all have to be active for the message to get through from the source to the recipient as understood by the source.[181]

5.3.1 Methods of communication.

For dialogue to take place through the process of communication there are various means, most important is speech in various

---

[180] Haggai Institute (Singapore), Lecture notes on Communication, 1995.
[181] Haggai Institute (Singapore), Lecture notes on Communication, p. 95.

languages. These days communication through writing is becoming more and more important, and communication can also be achieved through non-verbal means.

In this process the audience is not just a group of passive recipients of the Good News; since they respond either negatively or positively. The fact is that human beings react to any message that comes to them. That is a characteristic of human behaviour. Therefore, if man reacts to every message that comes to him, the sender must always be aware of how the message is delivered by having in mind the type or nature of the audience he/she is dealing with.[182]

5.4 Methods for effective communication

There could be varieties of methods of approach but for our purpose two approaches shall apply either for ineffective or effective results of the message to reach the intended goal as intended by the sender. These can be clarified as follows:-

5.4.1 Deductive approach

In the deductive approach the sender or source or messenger bears all authority to pass on the message and gives no room for discussions or questions for clarity. That means the message given must be accepted as it is. In this respect, the recipient is not given room or freedom of expression even on those issues that are not understood; his duty is to accept and act accordingly.[183]

5.4.2 Inductive approach.

The inductive approach, however, demands 'give and take', implying that there is the possibility of discussion. The recipient is able to explain his case while the sender is able to reason together with the recipient where the message is not understood or is not clear enough. It is upon their deliberations that a resolution is

---

[182] Ibid.
[183] Ibid.

reached. Good Muslim - Christian relations promote communication to enhance dialogue because "the audience is not just a group of passive recipients."[184]

5.5 Mission

The Concise Oxford Dictionary defines the word 'mission' - for our purpose - as:

> "A body sent by a religious community to propagate its faith, field of missionary activity, missionary post, organization in a district for conversion of the people; course of religious services etc."[185]

One may still ask; what is mission? Who are missionaries? Where are the mission fields?[186]

There are various views to explain the term 'Mission'. Some say it is a special undertaking by interested people or groups; a matter of spreading western civilization or western imperialism; or spread by violent methods rather than by loving service or emphasizing the planting of churches or heroic willingness to sacrifice when every other religion is bitterly fought as demonic. If our definition can only be based on the above then it falls short because it has its own weaknesses.[187]

This may probably mislead us to think that only the whites were or are eligible for being called missionaries because they come from the western civilization. The word Mission should remind us of the Gospel – the Good News – of Jesus Christ sent to us from God to live among us. It is when we have this truth that we are able to define the word. The word mission in short is the primary source for missiology – 'the study of mission'.

---

[184] Ibid.
[185] Ibid.
[186] *The Concise Oxford Dictionary*, Oxford University Press, 1966, p. 775.
[187] D.S. Mwakanandi, *Missiology*, TEEM Workbook (Zomba: nd.), p. 6.

Therefore, mission is witnessing for the kingdom of God as Jesus says, "The kingdom of God is here."[188] Later on, Jesus repeats the statement saying, "The kingdom of God is among you."[189] Further, Jesus says, "You will be my witnesses."[190]

In this respect, we can deduce that mission is the propagation of salvation found through Jesus Christ or the conscious attempt to propagate the Christian faith. William Carey in 1792 argued that "Mission is the use of means for the conversion of the heathens"[191] Others would say that mission happens by unconscious influence exercised on others or by spontaneous expansion of the community of faith.

Ultimately the word 'mission' must be defined in reference to God himself, so we speak of *Missio Dei*, the mission of God. The acceptance of the belief in God originates from God Himself through his works as portrayed through creation, and through his saving acts in Jesus Christ who was born human and lived among us as one of us and yet He is God.

In the epistle to the church in Philippi, Paul writes that Jesus emptied himself to become like us and lived among us, to reveal the great love of God to the whole of the creation and in particular man, created in His own image.[192]

Thirdly, God reveals his power of sustaining man and his creation through the Holy Spirit; to convict, to care and to guide the saved ones. Therefore, when we talk of mission, we refer to God as the initiator of the whole process in order to reveal himself to man so that man may make a choice to reject or accept Jesus as Lord and Saviour. So the essence of the Gospel is that humankind should be reconciled to God for his glory. God is holy and pure while man is sinful. But even then God uses man as a means. That is why human

---

[188] Matthew 4:17 (RSV).
[189] Luke 17:21 (RSV).
[190] Acts 1:8.
[191] Mwakanandi D.S., *Missiology*, TEEM Workbook (Zomba: nd.), p. 6.
[192] Philippians 2:1-11 (RSV).

tendency is likely to appear once in a while but the essence of the Gospel remains intact for the salvation of mankind.[193]

The Afrikaans proverb says,

"With a crooked stick you can kill a snake."

That means nothing is impossible with God. He uses fallen man to extend his kingdom. The inter-faith dialogue began with God himself, for he does not force people to follow him or accept him or else; he does not have an army that forces people to obey him. That is why evil people sometimes appear to prosper by earthly standards compared to the sincere children of God. This began in the Garden of Eden. Adam and Eve disobeyed God and God told them 'you shall die'.[194] Man was given freedom of choice either to choose good or evil, and Adam and Eve chose evil.

Man's life is full of choices but God always reveals the consequences of every choice that an individual takes. This is true in dialogue, for both parties state their view points and any individual is free to make a decision whether to accept or not.[195] For example, Paul talks to the Athenians of the unknown God in Acts 17:23. He comes to them without condemnation but appreciates what they know of the unknown.

The last example is that of Jesus Christ. Being born human, he performed miracles to reveal the secrets of the kingdom of God; but he left the choice for man to accept him or not.

5.6 Guidelines to dialogue.

Dialogue as a pre-requisite for Malawi Muslims and Christians must be understood in the context that dialogue is not discussing

---

[193] For example in the early missionary era, Africans were barred to wear hats or shoes in the mission stations or churches. This was common among the early Nkhoma Synod missionaries. Such a practice is contradictory to the Good News found in Jesus, but the cross was so and still is powerful to save mankind despite the weaknesses in the vessels that God uses.

[194] .Mwakanandi D.S., *Missiology*, TEEM Workbook (Zomba: nd.), p. 9.

[195] Genesis 2:1ff (RSV).

religious or theological subjects. Neither is it a polemical agenda with the ultimate goal of defeating the other nor is it confrontational, for it is not a debate but rather a conversation on a common subject between two or more people with differing views.

The aim of dialogue is to learn from each other so that change and growth in understanding of the other is achieved, unlike what took place in history, when a confrontational and more polemical approach was practiced with the ultimate goal of defeating the other because one party was convinced that "it alone had the absolute truth."[196]

In dialogue each partner has to listen to the other party with a clear mind, sympathetically with love as much as he is able to have, in an attempt to understand the other's position as precisely and, as it were, as much from within as possible. Such an attitude automatically includes the assumption that at any point, one might find the partner's position so persuasive that, if we are sincere with ourselves, we have to change though change is disturbing.

L. Swidler lays out ten principles for dialogue to take place which of course are not theoretical rules but have come about through hard experience as recaptured by Sigvard von Sicard in the report of a seminar on Christian – Muslim relations as highlighted below,[197]

1. The sole purpose of dialogue is to learn, change and grow into a new understanding. Dialogue is not to force change on one's partner as it is always the case in debates but change must only come after understanding and with a new perception of issues.
2. Dialogue is a two-sided project in interfaith issues and so requires it to occur within each religious community or between religious communities for it is corporate in nature. In which case co-religionists must participate to

---

[196] Such an attitude was shown when the Pope proclaimed a crusade to capture Jerusalem, Antioch and the Holy Land in 1095.
[197] L. Swidler, "The Dialogue Decalogue, Ground Rules for Inter Religious, Inter Ideological Dialogue," *Journal of Ecumenical Studies*, Winter 1983, revised 1984.

share fruits and experiences which will eventually help the community to learn, change and then move forward to more perceptive insights into reality.
3. Each party or participant must come to the dialogue with complete honesty and sincerity: That means false fronts have no place in dialogue because where there is no trust there is no dialogue.
4. Inter-religious dialogue must not be concerned with a comparison of the ideals of one's own tradition compared to the reality of the partners' tradition: The comparison has to concern the ideals or practices of each of the dialogue partners.
5. The participants must define themselves: For example, only a Muslim can define from inside what it means to be a Muslim while others can describe what it looks like from the outside. Thus dialogue is a dynamic medium that participants learn, change and grow for their self-definition which will deepen, expand and get modified. It is of paramount importance that all dialogue partners define what it means to be authentic members of their own tradition.
6. Participants must come to the dialogue without any hard and fast assumptions as to where the points of disagreements are; that means partners should not only listen with open mind and sympathy but attempt to agree as far as possible, while maintaining integrity with their own tradition.
7. Dialogue is only possible between equals; therefore partners in dialogue must come to learn from each other as equals. That means the attitude of superiority must always be avoided at any cost.
8. Dialogue can only take place on the basis of mutual trust with a corporate dimension. That means starting from the known to the unknown.

9. Those who enter into inter-religious dialogue must be self-critical of both themselves and their own religious traditions. 'Lack of self-criticism' implies that one's own tradition is considered to have all the correct answers. Such an attitude makes dialogue not only unnecessary but impossible.
10. Each party or participant must eventually try to experience the partners' religious tradition from 'within'. Religious tradition is something of head, spirit, heart, whole individual and community. This implies 'a pass over' into another's religious experience and then coming back enlightened, broadened and deepened in understanding.

Bearing in mind of the above principles or guidelines, dialogue will be fruitful to the benefit of those engaged in it. This shall then give room for religious co-existence in diversity and in peace.

To conclude we need to remind ourselves that in witness through dialogue the preacher or evangelist is used to give out the message and only that; nothing more; in this case God alone is responsible for the conversion. We cannot limit God for he has his own mysterious ways to convert people (Isaiah 55:8).

Further, the attitude of Muslims may differ with context or region in Africa and for every individual person, community, nation or spiritual level. This demands the understanding that when strategies or methods are applied they may also differ in witnessing through dialogue depending on where one is living on the continent of Africa. For example, the way you would approach a Malawian Muslim community would not be the same way you would approach Moroccan Muslim community. In-order to have a successful ministry amongst Muslims one has to adjust first one's mindset. For it is extremely difficult if not impossible to evangelize Muslims without change of the mindset.

John Azumah, a Ghanaian Muslim converted to Christianity calls such the 'mindset of Jonah'. For Jonah thought that the people of Nineveh could not be converted and he compares that with even the non - Muslim areas; where it took years of toil for the Gospel to penetrate countries like Japan, China, Korea, India, to mention a few, and this would obviously not give exception of Muslim countries.[198] It is because of this mindset that sadly Muslims are or may be regarded as enemies and only good for the fire of hell (cf. Jonah 4:1-3). In this respect Muslims are not the problem but Christians because of their self-defeatist attitude.[199]

John Azumah adds that visible public presence of Christians as a witness in a Muslim neighbourhood is very vital. Islam is a very public religion, wherever we find a Muslim community, whether small or large, we will not fail to notice it because of the minaret, the call to prayer five times a day, the distinctive veil worn by women. Above all, he says, "Islam is eaten daily." In the meat industry in Africa today in most cases, all animals for meat have to be slaughtered by a Muslim.[200] The public presence, probably, confirms the teaching of Jesus Christ about public witness, when he demands his followers to be like light, salt, leaven, or a city on a hill (Matthew 5:13-16). That is why effective witness must be in the language of the people and in the context of the people, so that they can understand through the medium they are able relate to, and not an accusation or a judgment.

Avoiding attacking Islamic beliefs and practices, the Quran or the person of Muhammad in our conversation with Muslims will enhance our witness. Judgmental or confrontational approaches are not suitable as means of witness and are not helpful at all. Instead, they turn Muslims to hostility and so they fail to listen to the Gospel, the Good News.

A question may arise: What shall we do in times when Muslims rise to hostility unnecessarily? In reply to such a question we should

---

[198] John Azumah, "*Christian Witness to Muslims: Rationale, Approaches and Strategies*", *Missionalia*, vol. 34, April 2006, pp. 6-18.
[199] J.T. Addison, *The Christian Approach to the Moslems: A Historical Study*, New York: Colombia University Press, 1942, p. 64.
[200] John Azumah, "*Christian Witness to Muslims: Rationale, Approaches and Strategies*", *Missionalia*, vol. 34, April 2006, pp. 6-18.

realize that we are not being timid or unaware of Muslim attacks on Christians nor do we avoid taking a critical view of Islamic teaching and history.[201]

Christians are duty bound to speak out against oppressive systems or violations of Human Rights. This is part of the prophetic vocation as Jesus says, "I am sending you out like sheep among wolves. Therefore, be as shrewd as snakes and as innocent as doves" (Matthew 10:16). So our role is to be witnesses (Acts 1:8).

John Azumah testifies, "Witnesses talk of things experienced, teachers develop ideas and doctrines but witnesses speak of the impact of these ideas and doctrines on their lives." Woodberry and Shubin say that the focus on the beauty of Jesus is also of paramount importance because the person and his acts are a powerful attraction to Muslims.[202] The Quran accepts Jesus' virgin birth though it sees him as an ordinary prophet, but still he is given mysterious titles such as Messiah, Word of God, Spirit of God. In addition, only Jesus alone was able to heal, to raise the dead, to create life, and Muslims believe that he will come again to restore peace in the world.

Some Muslim mystics present Jesus as a great prophet, a wandering monk preaching perfect poverty and love, while orthodox Muslim theologians see him just one prophet among many, while Muslim polemicists like Ahmed Deedat of South Africa tend to build a body of anti-Christian literature and sometimes make fun of Jesus.

It should be noted that one in every four Muslim converts to Christianity speaks of the role of the Jesus figure in their religious development, like Jesus appearing in dreams, visions and sometimes in direct personal encounters. Because of this

---

[201] John Azumah, "*Christian Witness to Muslims: Rationale, Approaches and Strategies*", Missionalia, vol. 34, April 2006, pp. 6-18.
[202] J.D. Woodberry and R.G. Shubin, *Why I Chose Jesus*, in http://www.missionfrontiers.org/2001/01/ muslim.htm (Feb. 2006):2001.

phenomenon we should not witness for Jesus as a dogma, for he is not a set of ideas. It takes God or Jesus himself to reveal Jesus' mysterious identity to people. Therefore, building and maintaining a relationship with the Muslims is more important than defeating him/her in an argument.[203]

Therefore, where there are Christians with a Muslim background we need to identify, disciple, train and support them and make use of the unique insights of the Muslim background they have as the speak the same language and share the same culture. Sometimes Muslim converts become outcasts in their communities upon becoming followers of Jesus, but in the sub-Saharan region they are usually re-accommodated.[204] The church can make use of the converts once discipled and harvest more because they are known to their own people. For example the Samaritan woman came to Jesus with a harvest of souls upon hearing the message of Jesus from her because they heard the message from the one whom they knew as one of them (John 4:1-42, 10:5). That means the Gospel has to be clothed with tolerance, love, humility, compassion, justice, equality etc (Galatians 5:22) in order to bear fruit for God.

---

[203] John Azumah, "Christian Witness to Muslims: Rationale, Approaches and Strategies", *Missionalia*, vol. 34, April 2006, pp. 6-18.
[204] Ibid.

Picture no. 1: What do you see in the picture? (Look closely before you proceed.)

Picture no. 2: What do you see in the picture? (Look closely before you proceed.)

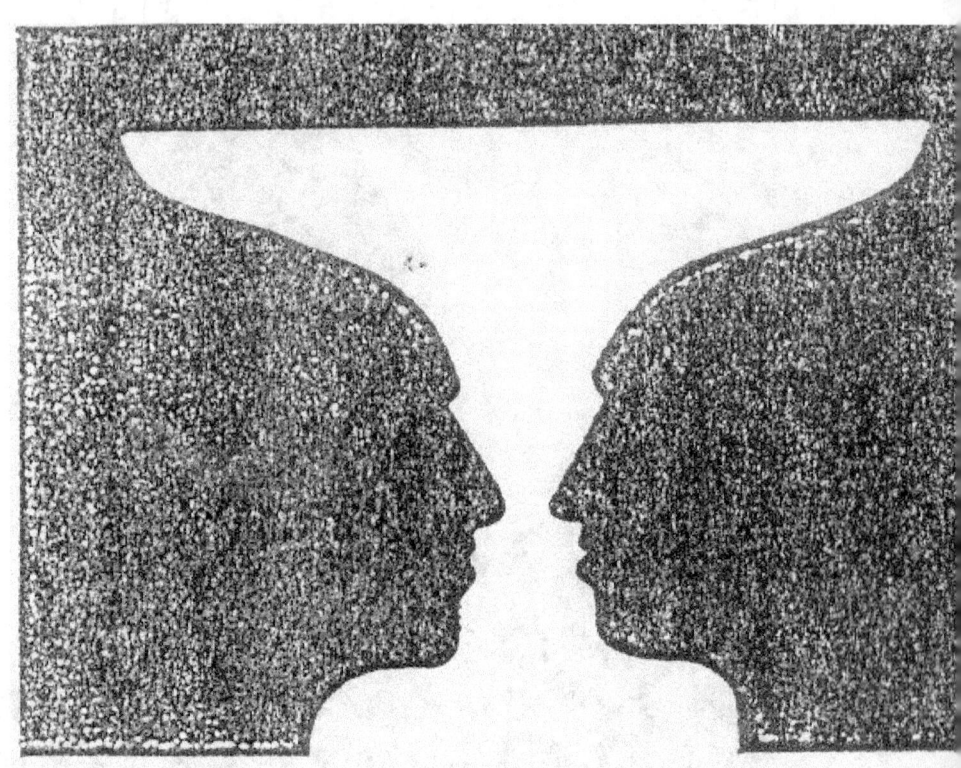

CHAPTER SIX

Conclusion

This book establishes that Malawians in the area researched have deeper roots in African Traditional Religions than in the expatriate religions in regard to Islam and Christianity. This could probably be true in that religious pluralism in African context remains acceptable in the minds of the Africans. Therefore, this phenomenon may be true for the people of Dedza northwest and Lilongwe east. And this African attitude initiates good neighbourliness in diversity.

Although the research has been limited to Dedza northwest and Lilongwe east therefore it cannot be generalized for the whole Malawi but as a model; leaving us with a lot of challenges if we would want to establish something tangible and concrete for the whole of Malawi. This is so because there are so many areas that needs to be researched on like the eastern region which comprise Mangochi, Machinga, Zomba and part of Ntcheu districts where the predominant population is of Yao tribe and most of whom are Muslims.

Another area that would require research in the Central Region is along the lakeshore from Nkhotakota, Salima, part of Dedza and Ntcheu district which have also a high percentage of Muslims. In addition we have Karonga district in the north where Muslim communities are also to be found not forgetting Chiradzulu, part of Mulanje and Blantyre districts where we may also find Muslim population. In this case we cannot forget all urban and semi-urban areas where we have Muslim communities in sight.

Then, looking at the vastness of the area not researched on yet; we cannot compare the findings of Dedza northwest and Lilongwe east to the vastness of Malawi. Therefore, the slice of Dedza northwest and Lilongwe east cannot determine the position of the whole Malawi. If we may want to have something concrete and tangible for Malawi as a nation on the two religions on interaction, there is need for doing further extensive research for another book.

Lastly, we can see how PROCMURA's approach was established, the only African organization born in Africa and works for the good of both Muslims and Christians in Africa for it believes in the equality of humanity. The other advantage is that Africans are a community people therefore, with of PROCMURA's teaching that emphasizes equality of humanity lays a base for Africans. In addition we discover that Africans tend to cherish African heritage more than foreign ideologies and so in this venture is from known to unknown and so makes it easier to establish interfaith dialogue. Another challenge is that though the University of Malawi introduced Islam in its curriculum but still more needs introducing Christian Muslim Relations as a subject that Malawians would benefit and have effect on the elite by making it easier to work with people at grassroot level. Therefore, with the establishment of Public Affairs Committee (PAC) and Malawi Interfaith Aids Association (MIAA) they stand as a base for interfaith dialogue.

The book reveals that doctrinal issues in the area do not pose much of a threat at all, to effect the unity of the people at grassroots level. Muslims and Christians are accommodating to each other. This is the attitude the CCAP Nkhoma Synod has towards Muslims and encourages other churches to work ecumenically. For example, CCAP Nkhoma Synod works together with the above named organizations, which promote the interfaith dialogue in diversity for peaceful co-existence.

In light of these findings the attitude of dialogue is very important as catalyst for witnessing for one's religion. This will then bring about a change of mindset, for God is upon all his people to his glory. In this context Muslims and Christians would live in religious diversity yet in peace.

Bibliography.

Oral informants through interviews

Lobi Mosque views on Muslim – Christian relations, 08/2003.
Mayani Mosque views on Muslim – Christian relations, 08/2003.
Monekera CCAP views on Christian – Muslim relations, 08/2003.
Monekera CCAP views on Christian – Muslim relations, 08/2003.
Chawa CCAP, Session views on the Christian – Muslim rations, 08/2003.
Mfumu (Village Headman), Chitundu CCAP views on Christian – Muslim relations, 08/2003.
Chitundu CCAP views on the Christian – Muslim rations, 08/2003.
Chitundu CCAP views on Christian – Muslim relations, 08/2003.
Dangaya ,Personal views on the Christian – Muslim rations, 08/2003.
Mayani Mosque views on Muslim – Christian relations, 08/2003.
Mayani Mosque views on Muslim – Christian relations, 08/2003.
Mayani Mosque views on Muslim – Christian relations, 08/2003.
Kajawa, M.J., Personal Interview on Christian – Muslim relations, 08/2003.
Kaliza, H.L.C., Mnthandiza CCAP views on Christian – Muslim relations, 10/2001; 08/2003.
Chitundu CCAP views on the Christian – Muslim relations, 08/2003.
Kamenya, S.J., Mphunzi CCAP views on Christian – Muslim relations, 10/2001.
Chitundu CCAP views on the Christian – Muslim rations, 08/2003.
Chawa CCAP views on Christian – Muslim relations, 08/2003.
Madalitso CCAP views on the Christian – Muslim rations, 08/2003.
Chawa CCAP views on the Christian – Muslim rations, 08/2003.
Mayani Mosque views on Muslim – Christian relations, 08/2003.
Chawa CCAP views on Christian – Muslim relations, 08/2003.
Monekera CCAP views on Christian – Muslim relations, 08/2003.
Linthipe Mosque, views on Muslim – Christian relations, 08/2003.
Mustafa, Mayani Mosque views on Muslim – Christian relations, 08/2003.
Monekera CCAP views on Christian – Muslim relations, 10/2001; 08/2003.
Chawa CCAP views on Christian – Muslim relations, 10/2001.
Linthipe Mosque views on Muslim – Christian relations, 08/2003.
Mkuka, E.J., Personal views on the Christian – Muslim rations, 08/2003.
Chitundu CCAP views on Christian – Muslim relations, 08/2003.
Monekera CCAP, Session on views on the Christian – Muslim rations, 08/2003.
Chitundu CCAP views on Christian – Muslim relations, 08/2003.
Nkhoma CCAP, Session views on the Christian – Muslim rations, 08/2003.
Chawa CCAP views on Christian – Muslim relations, 08/2003.
Mnthandiza CCAP views on the Christian – Muslim rations, 08/2003.
Lobi Mosque views on the Muslim – Christian Relations, 08/2003.
Sasu, A.A., Nkhoma Synod Offices, Likuni, views on Christian – Muslim relations, 08/2003.

Thete Mosque views on the Muslim – Christian Relations, 08/2003.
Thete Mosque views on Muslim – Christian relations, 10/2001.
Zintambira, A.R., Mnthandiza CCAP views on Christian – Muslim relations, 08/2003.
Unpublished material.
Azumah, John, The Legacy of Arab Islam in Africa: A Quest for Inter-religious Dialogue, 2001.
Bakatuinamina, Bulabuba Sebastien,"When African says 'Allah' – The Significance of the African World View Shaping Islam in Africa," PhD, University of Birmingham, 1994.
Brown, Stuart E., Project for Christian – Muslim Relations in Africa - Minutes of the 38th Executive Committee Meeting, Centre Chappoulie: Yopougon, Côte D'Ivoire, 1998.9.25.
CCAP General Assembly, HIV/AIDS Policy, 'Love, Care and Compassion, Head Office, Lilongwe, 2004.
Chakanza, J.C., A Brief Survey of Christian – Muslim Relations in Malawi 1875-1990, Paper read at the Theological Consultation on Christian – Muslim Relations and the Teaching of Islam in Institutions in Eastern Africa, presented in Nairobi-Kenya, 23rd -26th April, 1990.
Christian Council of Malawi, Council minutes, 1972.
Kalagho, Bertha, Minutes of Area Committee Meeting at Chilema CLTC 10th May, 2001.
Kaufa, Andrew U., Muslim – Christian Dialogue: A Challenge to Christian Churches in Malawi, Dipl, University of Malawi, 1993.
London Mission League of Arab States, volume 1 issue 2, ARABFILE, August 1993.
Mnthambala, A.J.M., *The Role of the Church in Christian – Muslim Relations in Malawi*, Pretoria:Rand Africaans University, 1993, unpublished.
Mnthambala, A.J.M., *Muslim Presence: Interactions with African Traditional Religion and its Relation to Christianity: A Case Study of Malawi*, PgD, University of Birmingham, 1998.
Mnthambala, Anderson J.M., Study Tour Report 1997/98 Academic Year at Westhill College (University of Birmingham-UK) to Malawi Council of Churches, 30.10.1998.
Malango, Bernard A., 'The Cross and the Crescent: their Meeting Point'. M.A. Irish School of Ecumenics – Dublin University, 1995.
Musopole, A.C., Letter of appointment to the post of Area Advisor-Fr. E. Malunda.-Malawi Council of Churches (honorary), 2002/02/20.
Mwakanandi, D.S., *Missiology*, TEEM Workbook (Zomba: nd.), p. 6.
Namwera, Leonard (ed), ECM Newsletter, ECM Mass Communication Department, Catholic Secretariat, February, 1997.
Neighbour Mission Committee, NMC, Neighbour Mission Committee Minutes, 2/02/06.

Nielsen, S.J., Forms and Problems of Legal Recognition for Muslims in Europe. Research Papers no. 2: Christian – Muslim Relations - Selly Oak Colleges, Birmingham 29, UK, June 1979.

Nkhoma Synod CCAP, Minutes, 1993.

Nkhoma Synod CCAP, Synod Mission Policy, 1999 p. 7.

Nkhoma Synod CCAP, The General Secretary's Office, The Visitor's Book.

Nkhoma Synod Minutes, Mission Policy for Christian – Muslim Relations and the Evangelism of our Neighbour, 18-25/10/1999.

Oduyoye, Modupe: Decision of the Executive Committee of PROCMURA on the Evaluation of the Project for Christian – Muslim relations at 38th PROCMURA Meeting, minutes 1997-11:24-25,

Phiri, Robert, Public Affairs Committee Report 2003, p. 5.

PROCMURA, PROCMURA Newsletter, no 58, 2003.

Stammer, F. Joseph and Sem Chipenda Dasonkho, Final Report - Evaluation of the Project for Christian – Muslim Relation in Africa, November 17, 1997.

Woodberry, J.D. and R.G. Shubin, *Why I Chose Jesus*, http://www.missionfrontiers. org/2001/01/muslim.htm (Feb. 2006:2001).

Christian Council of Malawi - AGM Minutes 8-9th May 1967.

CCM –Annual General Meeting Minutes-	6-8 November, 19673.
CCM – AGM - Minutes	5 November, 1969.
CCM- AGM Minutes	4-5 May 1971.
CCM – AGM - Minutes	14/11/1971.
CCM-AGM - Minutes	3-4 May 1972. .
CCM –AGM Minutes	2/11/1972.
CCM - AGM	30th April -1st May, 1974.
CCM – AGM Minutes	7-8th May, 1975.
CCM AGM Minutes	5-6th May 1976
CCM - AGM Minutes	4-5th My, 1977.
CCM –AGM Minutes	2-3rd My, 1978.
CCM – AGM Minutes	9 -10th May1979
CCM – AGM Minutes	10-11 June, 1980.

Kaufa Andrew U., Muslim-Christian Dialogue: A Challenge to Christian Churches in Malawi, Dipl. University of Malawi, 1993.

Mnthambala Anderson J.M., Study Tour Report 1997/98 Academic Year at West hill College

(University of Birmingham-UK) to Malawi Council of Churches 30 / 10 / 1998.

Neighbour Mission Committee, NMC, Neighbour Mission Committee Minutes, 2/0206.

Nkhoma Synod CCAP Minutes, Mission Policy for Christian - Muslim Relations and the Evangelism of our neighbour, 18-25/10/1999.

Kalao Bertha, Minutes of the Area Committee Meeting at Chilema CLTC 10th May, 2001.

Published Materials

Abdullah, Yusuf Ali, *The Meaning of the Holy Quran. Revised Translation*, Amana Publications, 1996.

Abbot, Walter M., S.J., *The Documents of Vatican II*, New York: The America Press, 1966.

Addison, J.T., *The Christian Approach to the Moslems: A Historical Study*, New York: Colombia University Press, 1942.

Alpers, Edward A., "Towards a History of the Expansion of Islam in East Africa: the Matrilineal Peoples of the Southern Interior," in: David S. Bone (ed.), *Malawi's Muslims. Historical Perspectives*, Blantyre: CLAIM-Kachere, 2000.

Arens, W., "Islam and Christianity in sub-Saharan Africa: Ethnographic Reality or Ideology", *Cahiers d' Etudes Africaines*, vol. 15, 1975.

Azumah, John, "Christian Witness to Muslims: Rationale, Approaches and Strategies", *Missionalia*, vol. 34, April 2006, pp. 6-18.

Blignaut, Chris, *Nkhoma Synod CCAP. Museum* brochure, Nkhoma: Nkhoma Synod, nd.

Bone, David S. (ed.), *Malawi's Muslims. Historical Perspectives*, Blantyre: CLAIM-Kachere, 2000.

Bone, David S., "An Outline History of Islam in Malawi", in David S. Bone, *Malawi's Muslims: Historical Perspectives*, Blantyre: CLAIM-Kachere: 2000, pp. 13-26.

Bone, David S., "Modernists and Marginalization", in: David S. Bone (ed.), *Malawi's Muslims. Historical Perspectives*, Blantyre: CLAIM-Kachere, 2000, pp. 69-88.

Bone, David S., "The Development of Islam in Malawi and the Response of the Christian Churches c. 1860-1986" in David S. Bone (ed.), *Malawi's Muslims. Historical Perspectives*, Blantyre: CLAIM-Kachere, 2000, pp. 113-153.

Braswell, George W., *Islam. Its Prophet, Peoples, Politics and Power*, Broadman & Holman, 1996.

Chakanza J.C. and Ross Kenneth R. (eds.), Religion in Malawi: Annotated Bibliography, CLAIM (Blantyre-Malawi):1998.

Chakanza J.C.(ed.), *Islam Week in Malawi,* Zomba: Kachere, 1998.

Chakanza J.C., and Hilary Mijoga, "Muslim Perspectives on Power", in: Kenneth R. Ross (ed.), *God, People and Power in Malawi. Democratization in Theological Perspective*, Blantyre: CLAIM-Kachere, 1996, pp. 125-148.

Chakanza J.C., and Kenneth R. Ross, *Religion in Malawi. An Annotated Bibliography*, Blantyre: CLAIM-Kachere, 1998.

Chakanza, J.C., "Christian - Muslim Co-existence and Development in Malawi," *African Ecclesiastical Review,* vol 44, nos 3 and 4, 2002, Eldoret AMECEA: Gaba Publications.

Chisale, Mattar V.K., "NAMS: Its Role and Impact on Muslim Students in Malawi From 1982 – 2005" BA Theology, University of Malawi 2006, Kachere Documents no. 17.

Chisoni Chris, Jere Tobious, Kuppens Jos and Swann Celia (eds.), Dialogue between Religions-Essential steps for Development, Zomba: Kachere, 2005

Coniaris, Anthony M., *The Orthodox Church. Its Faith and Life*, Minneapolis: Light and Life Publishing: Minneapolis, 1982, pp. 47-55.

Daudi, Amadu, "The Role and Impact of Munazzamat Al-Dawa-Al-Islamia Schools in Malawi from 2000-2006, A Case Study of Zomba and Mangochi Secondary School as Salam Boys As Salam Girls Al-Bakr and Aisha Girls Secondary School" BA Theology, University of Malawi 2006, Kachere Documents no. 35.

Deedat, Ahmed, *Is the Bible God's Word?* Durban: IPCI, 1992.

Esack, F. "Worship in a South African Prison Cell", *Interfaith News*, no. 10, February, 1980.

Fiedler Klaus, *Teaching Church History in Malawi*, Zomba: Kachere, 2005.

Fiedler, Klaus, "Islamization in Malawi – Perceptions and Reality", in Klaus W. Müller (ed.), *Mission im Islam. Festschrift für Bernhard Tröger*, Nürnberg: VTR, Bonn: VKW, 2007, pp. 252-262.

Fiedler, Klaus, "The Process of Religious Diversification in Malawi: a Reflection on Method and a First Attempt at a Synthesis", *Religion in Malawi,* no. 11, 2004.

Gilchrist, John, *Crucifixion of Christ: A Fact, not Fiction*, Cape Town: Life Challenge, 1985.

Gitau, Mary, Dogbe Angele Amole, *PROCMURA-SIRCA*, Africa Church Information Press, 2003.

Guillaume A., *The Life of Muhammad, A Translation of Ibn Ishaq Siart Rasul Allah*, Oxford: Oxford University Press: 1955.

Haqq, A., *Sharing the Lord Jesus Christ with Muslim Neighbours*, 1987.

Hofmeyr, A.L., "Islam in Nyasaland", *Moslem World*, vol 2 (1912), pp. 3-8, reprinted in David S. Bone (ed.), *Malawi's Muslims. Historical Perspectives*, Blantyre: CLAIM-Kachere, 2000, pp. 165-172.

Johnson, William Percival, "Mohammedanism and the Yao", *Central Africa*, vol. 29, 1911, pp. 57-61, 101-105, reprinted in David S. Bone (ed.), *Malawi's Muslims. Historical Perspectives*, Blantyre: CLAIM-Kachere, 2000, pp. 173-180.

Kalilombe, Patrick A., *Doing Theology at the Grass-roots. Theological Essays from Malawi,* Gweru: Mambo-Kachere, 1999.

Kateregga, Badru D. and Shenk David W., *A Muslim and a Christian in Dialogue*, Ibadan: Daystar, 1980.

Kirk, Andrew J., *What is Mission? –Theological Explorations*, London: Darton Longman and Todd, 1999.

Lamin, Sanneh, Piety and Power- Muslim and Christians in West Africa, Maryknoll: Orbis, 1996.

Leith, John H., (ed.), Creeds of the Churches, 'A Reader in Christian Doctrine from the Bible to the Present, Westminster: John Knox Press, 1982.

Lenning, L.G., Blessing in Mosque and Mission, Pasadena: William Carey Library, 1980.

Lewis, I.M., Islam in Tropical Africa, Oxford University Press, 1964.

Linden, Ian, Catholics Peasants and Chewa Resistance in Nyasaland, Los Angeles: University of California Press, 1974.

Lubbe, G., "Interfaith Dialogue in a Conflict Situation: The South African Scene," Discernment, vol. no. 2, Autumn 1986.

Matiki, Alfred J. "Problems of Islamic Education in Malawi", in: David S. Bone (ed.), *Malawi's Muslims. Historical Perspectives*, Blantyre: CLAIM-Kachere, 2000, pp. 154-16, earlier published in *Religion in Malawi* no. 4, 1994, pp. 18-22.

Matiki, Alfred J., "The Social and Educational Marginalization of Muslim Youth in Malawi", *Journal of Muslim Minorities*, vol. 19, no. 2, 1999.

Mbiti, John S., *Introduction to African Religion*, Nairobi: Heinemann, 1978.

McCracken John, Politics and Christianity in Malawi 1875-1940-The Impact of the Livingstonia Mission in the Northern Province, Cambridge University Press: 1997.

McCracken, John, *Politics and Christianity in Malawi 1875-1940*, Blantyre: CLAIM-Kachere, 2000.

McDonald, Roderick J., *From Nyasaland to Malawi. Studies in Colonial History*, Nairobi: EAPH, 1975.

Milazi, Ibrahim, "The Burning of Mosques in the North: Is it the Beginning or Climax of Political Fanaticism or of Christian Fundamentalism in Malawi?", *Religion in Malawi* no 9 (1999), p. 42.

Ministry of Justice, The Constitution of the Republic of Malawi, Malawi Government Press: Zomba, 2004.

Mohamad, Imuran Shareef, "Shura (Islamic Political Representation): Islamic and Western Perspectives, *Religion in Malawi,* vol. 11, 2004, pp. 12-18.

Mohamad, Imuran Shareef, "The Development of Tariqas in Malawi: Qadiriyah, Shadhiliyah and Sukuti", *Religion in Malawi,* vol. 10, 2000, pp. 19-24.

Mohamed, Imuran Shareef, "HIV/AIDS: An Islamic Perspective and Response", *Religion in Malawi,* vol. 12 (2005), pp. 10-14.

Nehls, Gerhard, Al-Kitab. A Bible Correspondence course for Muslims, Wellington: Biblecor, 1985.

Nehls, Gerhard, Christians Ask Muslims, London: Longman, 1973.

Nimts, H., *Islam and Politics in East Africa*, Minneapolis: University of Minnesota Press, 1980.

Nkhoma Synod CCAP, Zolamulira (Rules and Regulations), Nkhoma Press, 1970.

Paas, Steven, *Beliefs and Practices of Muslims -The Religion of our Neighbours*, Zomba: Good Messenger Publications, 2006.

Pachai B., *Malawi. History of the Nation*, London: Longman, 1973.

Panjwani, Ibrahim A.G., "Muslims in Malawi" (1979), in: David S. Bone (ed.), *Malawi's Muslims. Historical Perspectives*, Blantyre: CLAIM-Kachere, 2000, pp. 182- 196.

Pauw, Martin C., *Mission and Church in Malawi. The History of Nkhoma Synod of the Church of Central Africa Presbyterian 1889-1962*, Lusaka: BPM, 1980.

Phiri, Desmond Dudwa, *History of Malawi: From Earliest Times to the Year 1915*, Blantyre: CLAIM, 2004.

Praetorius H.L., Odendaal A.A., Robinson P.J. and Van der Merwe G. (eds.), *Reflecting on Mission in the African Context*, Bloemfontein: Pro Christo, 1996.

PROCMURA, *Questions Muslims Ask*, ACIS Press, 2004.

PROCMURA, Witnessing in Religious Pluralistic Landscape in Africa, Strategic Plan 2007/8 - 2011/12.

Rajasheker, J. Paul (ed.), *Christian – Muslim Relations in East Africa*, Lutheran World Federation, 1988.

Ross, Andrew C., *Blantyre Mission and the Making of Modern Malawi*, Blantyre: CLAIM-Kachere, 1996.

Ross, Kenneth R., (ed.), *Christianity in Malawi: A Source Book*, Gweru: Mambo-Kachere: 1996.

Sicard, Sigvard von, Formal Meetings of Christian and Muslims in Africa, Bicmura, vol. 4, no. 3, 1969.

Swidler, L., "The Dialogue: Ground Rules for Inter-religious Inter-ideological Dialogue," *Journal of Ecumenical Studies*, Winter 1983/84, p. 4.

Swidler, L., The Dialogue Decalogue, Ground Rules for Inter Religious, Inter Ideological Dialogue, *Journal of Ecumenical Studies*, Winter 1983, revised 1984.

Temple, Arnold C., and Johnson A. Mbillah (eds.), *Christianity and People of other Faith Communities*, Africa Church Information Service (ACIS) Printing Press 2001.

Trimmingham, J. Spencer, *Islam in East Africa*, Oxford: Clarendon Press, 1964.

Walls, Andrew F., *The Cross Cultural Process in Christian History*, Maryknoll: Orbis, 2002.

Walls, Andrew F., *The Missionary Movement in Christian History. Studies in the Transmission of Faith*, Maryknoll: Orbis, 1996.

Wilson, G.H., *The History of the Universities Mission to Central Africa*, Letchworth: Garden City Press, 1935.

Appendix A:

Members of the Malawi Council of Churches.

The Council has twenty-two full and two affiliate member churches as follows: -
Diocese of Northern Malawi (Anglican).
Diocese of Lake Malawi (Anglican).
Diocese of Southern Malawi (Anglican)..
Diocese of Upper Shire (Anglican)..
CCAP Synod of Livingstonia..
CCAP Synod of Blantyre.
CCAP Synod of Nkhoma..
The African Methodist Episcopal Church.
The Zambezi Evangelical Church.
Churches of Christ..
Free Methodist Church.
Salvation Army.
Lutheran Church.
Evangelical Lutheran Church.
Baptist Convention of Malawi.
Evangelical Church of Malawi.
Providence Industrial Mission.
African Evangelical Church.
Independent Baptist Convention.
Church of Nazarene.
Seventh Day Baptists.
Baptists Convention of Malawi.
Church of Africa Presbyterian.
Methodist Church of Malawi.
Moravian (Affiliate status).
Pentecostal Assemblies of Malawi (Affiliate status).

Appendix B: PROCMURA :Malawi Area Committee.
The committee was instituted as follows:
Chairperson: Rev T. Mwambila-Livingstonia Synod CCAP
Vice: Rev Fr. George Ndomondo- Diocese of Southern Malawi.
Secretary: Mrs. Bertha Kalao- (Anglican) Diocese of Southern Malawi.
Vice: Rev D.R. H. Mtipela-CCAP Blantyre Synod.
Treasurer: Rev M.J. Sande-CCAP Blantyre Synod.
Vice: Rev Absalom L. Kasiya: Anglican Diocese of Southern Malawi.
Committee Members:
Rev A.J.M. Mnthambala-CCAP Nkhoma Synod. /Area Advisor Malawi-2003/02
Rev Butawo- Baptist-Lilongwe.
Rev Muwalo- Evangelical Church -Blantyre.
Rev Mabuwa -PIM (48).
This committee operates in Malawi to accomplish PROCMURA's vision. In matters of seminars on Christian – Muslim relations, the committee covers subjects like: -
History of Islam.
History of Christian – Muslim Relations.
Islam in Africa.
Witness and Dialogue.
Issues in Christian – Muslim Relations etc.

Appendix C: Institution of neighbour mission committee:

The second meeting took place on the 10th April, 1999 held at Msalula CCAP Congregation. The following office bearers were elected into their respective offices.

Rev J.L. Sankhani- Chairperson of Dzimvere gospel Service a member of Msalula CCAP

Rev Z. Dangaya- Vice of Kolowiro CCAP congregation

Mr. H.M. Chiwaula- of Nkhotakota CCAP

Mrs. C. Nyirenda- Vice Secretary/Treasurer of Msalula CCAP

Members

Ms. L. Laubscher – of Nkhoma CCAP (Hospital)

Mr. L.T. Mkuli- of Khola CCAP a converted Muslim

Mr. M.J. Chafulumira- of Msalula CCAP congregation

Rev M.J. Kafantenganji – The Pastor, Msalula CCAP

Rev Ryk Van Velden – Mission Secretary as ex-official (Member of Mission Committee of Synod).

Mr. C.G. Maenje – Deputy Mission Secretary Committee of Synod, ex – official (Member of mission committee Synod)

Appendix D: members of Programme for Christian – Muslim relations in Africa

Full Members

A-East Africa:

Kenya, Ethiopia, Uganda, Malawi, Sudan and Tanzania

B- West Africa

(i) Anglophone:

Gambia, Ghana, Sierra Leone, Nigeria- East, West and North Liberia.

(ii) Francophone: Ivory Coast, Togo, Benin, Burkina Faso and Senegal.

B-Members to become:

Zambia and Zimbabwe

D-Provisional Area Committees:

Guinea

E- Contacts:

Central African Republic, Cameroon, Madagascar, Mali, Niger, South Africa and Zaire

APPENDIX E: The PROCMURA strategic plan 2007/08 – 2011/12

The strategic plan presented and discussed fully at the workshop in January 2006 has really shown progress in this ministry. The first of its kind in the history of PROCMURA; it has a clear vision statement, mission statement, core values, and core objectives to mention a few. After minor corrections, adjustments and additions it was endorsed at the General Council held in August, 2007 in Ghana.

2.11.1 Vision statement

"Faithful and responsible Christian witness to the Gospel in an interfaith environment of Christians and Muslims, and Christian constructive engagement with Muslims for peace and peaceful co-existence for the holistic development of the human person and his/her environment."

2.11.2 Mission statement

"A Continent where faith communities, in spite of their differences, work together for the holistic development of the human family."

2.11.3 Guiding principles

PROCMURA as a Christian organization for Africa extends a hand of friendship to Muslim communities in the continent by maintaining faithful Christian witness as an integral part of Christian identity. It is involved in the constructive engagement between Christians and Muslims for peace and peaceful co-existence by following the example of Jesus Christ, who is himself the Prince of Peace. Therefore, PROCMURA

- Upholds and seeks a just and peaceful society for all.
- Affirms freedom of religion where everyone is free to practice their faith and co-exist with other faiths peacefully.
- Believes in the equality of all people.

- Believes as a Faith Based Organization (FBO), that truth and love are paramount values for peaceful co-existence.
- Mutual respect, good neighbourliness, and tolerance are acknowledged as critical components in the search for a peaceful, compassionate, and just world.
- Strives to serve as a resource pool for the churches to interpret the gospel faithfully in an interfaith environment of Christians and Muslims.[205]
- Believes in being a committed and accountable and transparent organization.
- Is committed to develop programmes and relations in accordance with acceptable Christian moral and ethical standards.
- Affirms the principle of partnership, collaboration and networking.

2.11.4 Overall goal

The overall goal for PROCMURA is to sensitize the Christian churches of Africa of their responsibility of understanding Islam and Muslims in relation to the churches interpreting the Gospel of Jesus Christ faithfully in the Muslim world by promoting constructive engagement with Muslims for peace and peaceful co-existence in society. PROCMURA's constitution provides the basis on how it should operate, providing a governance structure, management and organizational objectives as follows:-

- To encourage and facilitate research and education for the member churches.
- To help churches establish area committees as representatives of the churches in a given country, or in a region within a country to work with PROCMURA, a service in their respective areas.
- To subscribe to, assist, subsidize and co-operate with any organization or institution whose objectives are

---

[205] PROCMURA, Strategic Plan 2007/8 – 2011/12, pp. 13-14.

compatible with PROCMURA, and to subscribe to any funds, charitable or otherwise, deemed to promote the interest of the organization.
- To promote collaboration and coordination on matters relating to faithful Christian witness. PROCMURA shall act as a hub and reference to the churches and par-church communities in Africa and beyond without prejudice to its autonomy and what it stands for. And Christian constructive engagements with Muslims shall be enhanced for peace and peaceful co-existence.

2.11.5 PROCMURA's Niche

"PROCMURA is the sole Christian organization in Africa, dedicated to building mutual relationships between Christians and Muslims in the entire continent. Therefore, it is neither a multi-faith organization nor an interfaith one but a membership organization rooted in the church."[206]

---

[206] PROCMURA, Strategic Plan 2007/8 – 2011/12, pp. 13-14.

www.ingramcontent.com/pod-product-compliance
Lightning Source LLC
Chambersburg PA
CBHW051615230426
43668CB00013B/2112